MY BIG
FATHER

MY BIG FATHER

Dr Bruce Farnham

STL Books

PO Box 48, Bromley, Kent, England

PO Box 28, Waynesboro, Georgia, USA

PO Box 656, Bombay 1, India

ISBN 0 903843 89 7

STL Books are published by Send The Light (Operation Mobilisation),
PO Box 48, Bromley, Kent, England.

Covers printed by Penderel Press Ltd, Croydon, Surrey.

Printed and bound in Great Britain by Cox & Wyman Ltd., Reading

Contents

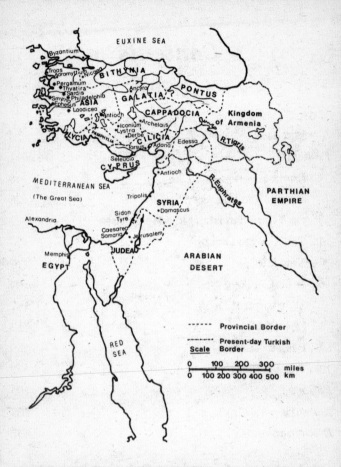

EUXINE SEA

Byzantium

Troas
Adramyttium Nicaea
Pergamum BITHYNIA
Thyatira Ancyra PONTUS
Smyrna Philadelphia Sardis GALATIA
Ephesus Laodicea
ASIA CAPPADOCIA Kingdom
of Armenia
Antioch
LYCIA Iconium Archelais
Lystra
PAMPHYLIA Derbe
CILICIA R. Tigris
Tarsus Adana Edessa
Seleucia
CYPRUS
MEDITERRANEAN SEA Antioch
R. Euphrates
(The Great Sea) PARTHIAN
EMPIRE
Tripolis
SYRIA
Sidon Damascus
Alexandria Tyre
Caesarea
Samaria Jerusalem
Memphis JUDEA ARABIAN
DESERT
EGYPT

```
- - - - -   Provincial Border

            Present-day Turkish
Scale       Border
0    100   200   300
                        miles
0  100 200 300 400 500
                        km
```

RED
SEA

NEW TESTAMENT TURKEY

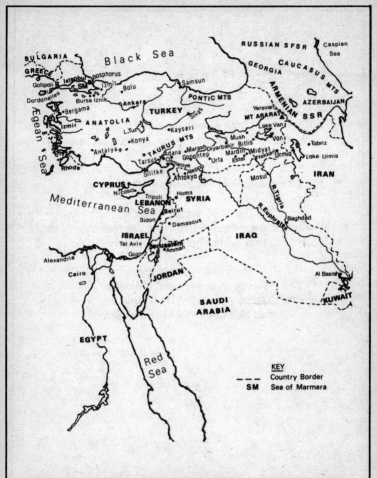

KENAN'S TURKEY

To Kenan's family
that they might know the joy that Kenan knew

To Jenny
who contributed so much to this account

To the Turkish Church
that it might grow founded firmly on the message of grace
that Kenan held to so clearly

And last, but not least,
To my dear wife and children
who graciously gave of their time and love
that this book might be written.

Introduction

My earliest memories of Kenan are from the summer of 1966 when I was visiting Turkey for the first time. I had just arrived in Istanbul, tired and dishevelled after hitch-hiking across Europe. Overwhelmed by the sights, sounds and smells of the bustling city, I landed on Kenan's door step late one sticky evening, a total stranger, to be greeted with a welcoming smile and a warm invitation to stay the night. It emerged that the timing of my visit was highly inconvenient; Kenan was working hard for exams the following day. Having just completed university exams myself a few days earlier, I was all the more impressed by his calm acceptance of this sudden intrusion upon his studies.

So began a friendship that continued for many years. After settling in Turkey with my family, we often used to visit Kenan and sit chatting over endless glasses of clear sweet tea, Kenan entertaining us from his apparently inexhaustible repertoire of Turkish jokes and stories.

There are several reasons why I want to make the story of Kenan more widely available. Firstly, it is impossible to talk about his life without telling something of the background and spiritual needs of Turkey and the Turks, a land and a people for which I hold a deep affection.

Secondly, I think I am not alone in feeling rather overwhelmed by the current surfeit of 'celebrity biographies'. While these make interesting reading, the lives of those they describe are often too remote from our own daily routine to be of more than passing relevance. Furthermore, the spirituality of many is so way beyond our own that we can readily become depressed rather than encouraged. The kingdom of God is about Jesus using very ordinary people to accomplish his purposes all over the world. Kenan was one of those who rejoiced to be such a foot-soldier in God's army.

Finally, Kenan had an infectious faith in his 'Big Father' – a great God who could and would act to provide for his children. It was the love of Kenan's 'Big Father' that drove him out of the ghetto mentality of his minority Christian community to share that love with as many as possible of the millions of Muslims around him.

For many people today, the world of Islam remains strange, unknown and threatening. As it was for Kenan, so it is for us – only as we see God as Father in all his heavenly power and glory will we be taken beyond our little worlds to become truly available to meet the needs of others.

Certain names have been changed in this account to maintain anonymity. Otherwise the events are, to the best of my knowledge, as they happened.

Prologue

London, 31 March 1971

A small woman with a brown weathered face and greying hair lay swathed in white on the operation table. Looking down from above, it seemed as if her slight body had been caught in a giant spider's web of shining tubes and brightly coloured electrode leads. The glare of theatre lights reflected off the jumble of instruments that surrounded her. The group of green-clad figures in surgical masks clustering round the table worked steadily and methodically, the silence broken only by the occasional terse command or the clatter of digital print-out machines linked to a battery of monitoring screens.

Moments earlier, as the grey-haired woman was lying on the trolley just before being anaesthetised, a doctor called Richard had held her hand and prayed with her. She spoke no English, but seemed to understand. As she was wheeled off she smiled and made a one-way sign pointing to heaven.

There was a pause in the operation. The chief surgeon carefully checked some clamps, and then reached down and lifted from the woman's abdomen a single kidney. This was the smaller of the woman's two kidneys. There was a murmur of approval from the group round the table. Far from being the mottled and blotchy organ so typical of older people, this kidney was red and shiny, the kidney of a girl, not of a woman who had given birth to ten children. Perhaps it was the clear air of her native village of Midyat, more than two thousand miles away in south-eastern Turkey. Perhaps it was that active life of daily drawing water from the well, and of bringing up a lively family of seven of those children, three having died in infancy. Perhaps it was the largely vegetarian diet, because meat was rare in the

Midyat of those days. Whatever the reasons, the surgeons
at St Mary's Hospital proclaimed it to be one of the heal-
thiest donor kidneys they had seen in all the 180 transplants they had performed up to that time.

A few paces down the corridor was another theatre. The
hair of the man on the operating table was jet-black with no
hint of grey, but his face was sallow and pinched, his body
wasted, and the group round this table was larger and
seemed more tense. They had already been working for
two hours, carefully closing off his wasted and diseased
kidneys, and preparing the crucial blood supply to be connected to a new kidney.

The man's name was Kenan Araz. The woman in the
theatre next door was his mother.

In a room not far away a girl sat thinking and worrying
and praying with a Christian nurse. She was Janet, Kenan's
sister. She had been fasting for twenty-four hours, but it
was hard to concentrate on prayer. She kept thinking of
cold sharp scalpels, and then her mind would wander to
her native Midyat, and she wondered whether her father
was worrying too, and what her sisters Habibe, Leyla and
Rashel were doing. In fact they had been fasting too, a complete fast without food and water for the past three days –
but today they were restless, wandering about the house,
waiting for the telephone to ring. Strong warm winds from
the Syrian deserts to the south blew across the rolling hills,
bringing down the remains of the almond blossoms and
rattling the window panes.

A nurse carefully placed the kidney taken from Mrs Araz
in a sterilised white dish and hurried to the adjoining
theatre. For a few moments part of her living body was sus-
pended in space, life gladly and willingly flowing out from
mother to son. Surrounded by the gleaming fruits of an ad-
vanced technological society were a mother, a son and a
sister from an unknown family from a small obscure village
in south-eastern Anatolia, in the middle of a rare operation,
one of the first such to have been carried out on anyone
from Turkey. The journey from the little village of Midyat to
the operating tables of a famous London hospital had been
very long indeed . . . .

1
Roots

Upper Mesopotamia, summer 1874

A cloud of dust and flies hung over the rough track as a pair of yoked oxen strained to pull a cart-load of heavy grey stone up the incline to 'Little Lake' on the outskirts of Midyat. In fact the lake in question only appeared in winter after the rains had begun and this summer, as every summer, there was only a shallow depression to mark the spot. But it was enough to give the area a name. The man prodding the struggling oxen up the slope was an 'Assyrian'. Several days' stubble masked a face burned deep brown by the sun, a long face with sloping forehead and arched bushy eyebrows set off by a distinctive curved nose and thick well-set lips. Isaiah was on his way to build a house. It was going to be a house that would last, built with the same heavy grey stone that characterised the rest of Midyat, helping the village to blend with the dusty hills around.

One day Kenan Araz would be brought up in the very same house. That time was still more than seventy years away, but his roots were here, buried deep in the village of Midyat.

The house was being built for the Protestant missionaries to serve as a base for a new evangelical work in the area. If it were possible for those silent slabs of stone, which Isaiah was putting into place with such care, to speak of the joys, hopes, fears and tragedies they were to witness in the tumultuous century ahead, the stones would surely have cried out their story.

By 1874, the missionaries had been visiting Midyat for more than ten years from their base in Mardin, fifty miles

across the rolling hills to the west. From the beginning
there had been hostility. Just as the Protestant
missionaries had been stoned and spat upon in the streets
of the much larger town of Mardin when they first moved
there in 1858, so visits to the Syrian Orthodox (or Jacobite)
village of Midyat had been marked by suspicion and
antagonism. Descriptions of the village by travellers at that
time are hardly flattering. In 1862 a missionary called Mr
Walker, who was carrying out a tour of the area, remarked
of Midyat:

> 'The population is entirely Jacobite; in character
> and conduct differing not a whit from the rude
> Koords around them; their relation to one another,
> even in the same village, being more in the way of
> **blood-feuds than anything else. The leaders of the**
> factions, although near relatives, dare not pass from
> their own quarter of the village to another without
> several attendants. Each desires to be acknowledged
> chief of the village; and each regards with deadly
> hatred whoever may secure this pre-eminence . . . .'

For years Dr Williams, the pioneer missionary in Mardin,
had fought to obtain a foothold in this divided village.
Though spiritually speaking the terrain hardly seemed
promising, Midyat was the administrative centre of about
one hundred Christian Jacobite villages in the area, and the
key to the mountains of the Jebel Noor beyond. On a clear
day the peaks could be seen rising up from the Tigris in the
east, icy and snowbound in winter, blue and hazy in
summer. While the rocky valleys and high plains were
traditionally the home of the mountain-dwelling Kurds,
there were also many Kurdish-speaking Muslim villages
intermingled with those of the Jacobites in the foothills
below. Midyat was therefore seen as a stepping stone to a
work amongst the Kurds.

The whole area was a patchwork of language, race and
religion. There were Sunni Muslims, Alevi Muslims whose
religion was similar to the Shiites of Iran, and the Yezidee,

who claimed to worship both God and the devil. Then there was a host of Christian Orthodox and Catholic churches jostling for power and influence. The Christian minorities of the Ottoman Empire had co-existed with their Muslim conquerors for centuries, living as separate *millets* (or *nations*) and exempt from military service on payment of a special tax. Though second-class citizens, many in fact held powerful positions in the Empire, particularly in those areas where Christians formed a large proportion of the population.

Mardin in the 1870s was just such a centre. An imposing town on the northern boundary of Mesopotamia , built high up on a hill 1,600 feet above the vivid greens of the great plain between the Tigris and the Euphrates, Mardin's half-Christian and half-Muslim population faithfully reflected the religious pot-pourri of the villages that surrounded it.

The ancient monastery of Deyr-ul-Zafaran, just a few miles from the city walls, and the even older monastery of Deyr-ul-Umur near Midyat (founded in 396 AD) were the ecclesiastical centres of the Syrian Orthodox Church in the area, otherwise known as the Jacobite Church. The Patriarch of the whole community, an impressive old man in black with a long flowing white beard, was based at Deyr-ul-Zafaran, and the Jacobites formed one of the largest Christian communities in Mardin. The Church traces its roots back to early Christianity in Antioch, but received its identity during the struggles to correctly define the human and divine natures of Christ during the church councils of the fifth century.

By the 1870s in Mardin there was also a sizeable community of Syrian Catholics, with their own Patriarch, formed by the efforts of Rome a century earlier to reunite the Syrian Orthodox with the Roman Catholic Churches, an effort that resulted in much division and bitterness. Add to this the Christian communities of Nestorians, Chaldean Catholics, Armenian Catholics and Gregorian Armenians living in the area, and it is small wonder that any Muslim on-looker should be confused as to where or even whether true Christianity could be found in this profusion of labels!

The first Protestant missionaries coming to live in Mardin in 1858 faced a baffling array of languages. Arabic was the general language of the area, but Turkish was the language of administration. There were two dialects of Kurdish, two of ancient Syriac, three of modern Syriac, and Armenian. The Jacobites celebrated their liturgy in ancient Syriac, an eastern dialect of Aramaic and very close to the language spoken by Jesus. The 'Assyrians' (called the Suryani by the Turks) were not really a separate race at all, but those belonging to the various churches in which the term 'Syrian' or 'Assyrian' was used. They spoke Syriac, Arabic or Kurdish, and many would know all three languages.

If the Muslim Turks found the various church labels confusing, some of the in-fighting between the many groups did even more to turn people away from the radical gospel of love preached by Jesus. Unlike other Turkish cities at that time, Mardin was not divided into distinct Muslim and Christian areas, so whatever happened in one community was immediately common knowledge in the other.

Jacobites who had seceded to Rome still worshipped in the same churches, but at different times. Sometimes fights would break out if the first group did not finish on time. Once these became so bad that the local *pasha* (or governor) heard of it and threw all the priests of the town indiscriminately into prison. The problem was finally solved by an extraordinary solution. A decree was obtained from Constantinople that every church should be divided in the middle by a wall, and that each party should take half. So for a time it was possible to attend services on one side of the wall, and hear the opposing group worshipping the same God on the other side.

The sterile stones of Mardin

It was into the midst of this complex mosaic of religious

tension and intrigue that the Protestant missionaries came. Some from Mardin's traditional churches were men of deep sensitivity, disgusted by the in-fighting around them, and they were quickly attracted to a message in which Christ was preached as one who came to break down dividing walls.

In an age generally characterised by syncretism and politely expressed bland theological opinions, it is difficult to grasp the intensity of religious feeling, loyalty and often plain fear that drove men of past generations to vicious religious disputes at one end of the spectrum and extremes of self-immolation at the other. One factor that did unite the churches of the area was that strong stream of Greek and essentially anti-biblical thought which declares that the aim of true religion is to subdue the body in order to free the soul for communion with God.

In the ancient monasteries near Mardin there was ample opportunity for the subduing of the body. Services that might last many hours took place at all times, day and night. Near the chapel of the Deyr-ul-Umur monastery, underground caves were used for times of lenten prayer and fasting, and sometimes monks would be walled into these places for weeks on end. Vertical slots just big enough to take one person were cut in the rock walls of the cave so that a monk could pray on his feet without danger of falling over because of fatigue or falling asleep. Under the floor of the cave and running its full length a further narrow space had been carved out. Here a monk could lie prostrate in the suffocating darkness to further his spiritual exercises.

One young monk called Baulus Bursam used to wear a belt with nails in it, the ends pointing inwards. He spent much time in one of these underground caves in the monastery at Midyat. He used to set up a rope such that, when sleep threatened to overcome him, he could fling himself across it so that he could keep awake to pray. As a result of Bibles being introduced into the monastery, Baulus came to a living faith in Christ by reading the

Scriptures for himself. Like Martin Luther centuries before, he suddenly saw that all his works were useless to bring him into the presence of a holy God. Coming into new freedom in Christ, his very first act was to throw away his nail-studded belt, but the scars remained with him for the rest of his life, until his martyrdom in 1896. In later years Baulus would show the scars to contrast the deadness of a religion of empty works with the full and complete salvation that is in Christ.

Complexities of religion and language were not the only challenges to face the first missionaries who came to the Mardin area. Though the town itself was relatively healthy due to its height above the plains, the whole area was subject to frequent drought, and for months all the spare time and energy of the new believers would be used in relief efforts. In 1864 the numbers of the small but growing church were decimated when seventeen members had to move to other areas to find work. In the same year typhoid claimed many lives, and in 1866 in Mardin there were 400 deaths from cholera. At another time all the crops and vineyards of the surrounding region, up to 10,000 square miles in area, were devastated by a plague of locusts. As if famine, drought and disease were not enough to make life arduous, plundering bands of Kurdish tribesmen would frequently descend from the mountains, robbing and burning surrounding villages, and carrying off a large number of livestock.

Somehow the physical hardship was reflected in the spiritual hardness of the people. Dr Williams was the sole missionary in the town in those early years and contrasted the 'stony, sterile stones' of Mardin with the spiritual renewal that was coming to many other areas of Turkey at that time. In the neighbouring towns of Gaziantep and Marash the gospel had broken into the large Armenian communities with astonishing results.

Expansion and opposition

Back in the 1840s an Armenian priest called Bedros had

been banished by his bishop from Constantinople to Jerusalem because of his evangelical views. In the event he never got nearer to Jerusalem than Beirut, and from there travelled back to Anatolia where he began a new work in Gaziantep amongst the town's Armenians. Within two years 200 families had professed Christ. It was a time when dire threats were being made from the Armenian Patriarch's pulpit in Constantinople against all Protestants. These culminated in a bull of excommunication issued on 25 January 1846, by which an evangelical priest called Vertanes, who had been boldly preaching the gospel from his own pulpit, was banished forever from the Gregorian Church. The bull is worth reading because it captures something of the intense and virulent opposition to the evangelical movement at that time from the established religious hierarchy, the evangelical movement at its inception still being part and parcel of the ancient Gregorian Church.

Before the bull was read, the patriarchal church in Constantinople was darkened by extinguishing the candles, and the great curtain was drawn in front of the main altar. The bull was then solemnly read out. The hapless Vertanes was described as 'a contemptible wretch' who 'following his carnal lusts' had forsaken the church. He was said to be a 'traitor and murderer of Christ, a child of the devil, and an offspring of Antichrist, worse than an infidel or a heathen' teaching 'the impieties and seductions of modern sectaries' (that is, *Protestants*). 'Wherefore we expel him and forbid him as a devil, and a child of the devil, to enter into the company of Believers'.

It is clear that the church dignitaries of mid-nineteenth century Constantinople were not yet familiar with the language of modern church diplomacy, and the bull was repeated the following Sunday, garnished with some further choice anathemas, only this time couched in words that effectively extended the excommunication to all those of Protestant belief in the Ottoman Empire.

The anathemas were carried out with great vigour, although the more violent acts were restrained by the direct intervention of Sir Stratford Canning, the British Ambassador to the Sultan. It was this patriarchal bull that led directly to the founding of the first Protestant church of the Ottoman Empire in Istanbul on 1 July, 1846.

The bull of excommunication was read in the churches of Gaziantep, but Bedros refused to be silenced, and an evangelical church was soon established there the following year. Though Bedros himself died from cholera two years later, his labour was not in vain, and the Gaziantep church grew rapidly. From the beginning it was a church with great missionary vision for the surrounding area. The members established their own local missionary society, and teams of young people went out to the surrounding towns and villages witnessing and distributing literature. Often they would go to Marash, but eleven times they were driven away with hails of stones. The church at Gaziantep also had a vision for a kind of missionary work which might today be more commonly known as 'tent-making':

> 'A novel experiment was made, early in the year 1849, to accomplish the object in view without subjecting themselves to the charge of being mere idlers, and "busybodies in other men's matters". Five individuals who had trades went forth to different towns, with their tools in one hand, and the sword of the Spirit in the other. Wherever they went they worked at their trade, while at the same time they laboured for the spiritual good of the people.'

In this way evangelical churches were planted in many of the surrounding towns and villages, and it was through a combination of such 'tent-making' and the continued outreach of evangelistic teams that the gospel first came to Marash. As in Gaziantep the seed, once taken, underwent extraordinarily rapid growth. In 1855 an evangelical

Armenian church was established with sixteen members. Within six years there were sometimes more than 1,000 at the Sunday morning service, with 1,500 more coming for the afternoon communion service. A local 'Soul Loving Missionary Society' had been established and was supporting five full-time workers. During those early days of expansion and revival there was little hint of the gruesome horrors that lay ahead for the believers of Marash.

Breakthrough at Mardin

But at Mardin things were different; everything seemed to go so slowly. Dr Williams plodded on. His wife died and was buried in the tiny cemetery near the mission compound, but he kept going. The breakthrough came in 1867 when a week of prayer was organised. The new believers had never shown much interest in prayer, but this week there was a sudden change of heart. Every morning at sunrise and every evening at sundown they met for prayer. The first meeting was held in pouring rain and thirty people came, the numbers building up as the week went on. Old wounds were healed, wrong relationships were put right, and the people began to pray 'as if they had done nothing else all their lives'.

As a direct result of this week of prayer the church was officially organised soon afterwards. The believers decided to appoint a full-time pastor and began to support him at the princely rate of four Turkish pounds a month. Nor was this all. Through prayer they caught a vision for the thousands of Kurds in the area who were almost totally unevangelised (even as they remain today), so they chose one of their own to be a missionary student who would later be sent out to work amongst these neglected people. He delighted in the name of Oosee Sit and was 'a great six feet, brawny fellow, with unwashed clothes [he was a tanner], long dishevelled hair, large open features, eyes black as coal, that shine like stars, but so simple in his trust,

so tender in his love of Jesus, so earnest in his efforts to do
good'. Sadly, no record remains of what happened to
Oosee; the last mention of him was as he waited for 'the
melting of the Taurus snows and the winding up of his
business to go and study, that he may preach the Jesus he
loves'.

A few months after the church was established, fierce
persecution broke out against the new Protestant
community. On the pretext that they had not paid the
correct taxes (a charge later shown to be false), many of
the Protestants were beaten and thrown into prison. Large
sums of money were extracted from each household,
equivalent to about a year's wages. Yet no one went back
on their new faith, and the trials united the believers as
never before.

Dr Williams died on 14 February, 1871, worn out at the
age of fifty-three by his long labours in the area. The church
at Mardin was not destined to grow like those at Gaziantep
and Marash, but a solid work had been started from which
ripples went out for hundreds of miles around, and the
church continued for fifty years until it was swallowed up
by the convulsions of the First World War.

Dr Williams was replaced by a younger man, Alpheus
Andrus. With the church in the hands of a local pastor,
Andrus was freer to organise outreach into surrounding
areas. With a special concern for the Kurds, he was soon
engaged in a translation of the New Testament into
Kurdish. It was this same love for the Kurds that pushed
him out again and again to the village of Midyat, the key to
the Kurds and the Jebel Noor beyond.

Advances in Midyat

And so we return to Isaiah the Assyrian, pulling heavy grey
stones up the slope outside Midyat. Isaiah was building a
house for the missionaries, to serve specifically as a base in
winter when travel from Mardin was frequently hindered
by mud or snow. For years the missionaries had hired a

room for meetings from Isaiah's father, and for some time now the room had been used as a school. Through this contact Isaiah had come to Christ. He was then the only known local believer from Midyat, the fruit of many years of prayer and concern for that area, the result of more than forty years of missionary outreach as the gospel had spread out from Constantinople, through Anatolia, in gradually widening circles.

So the grey stone house that gradually arose at 'Little Lake' on the outskirts of Midyat symbolised the laying down of lives, the battles in prayer, and the sweat and tears of many decades of hard missionary labour. Just as the heavy stones of the house could only be heaved into their correct positions with great effort, so each living stone of the emerging evangelical Church of the Ottoman Empire cost much before it could come into place in God's building.

It does not come as a surprise to read that the building of the house met with intense opposition. Indeed, progress was only possible because the local Kurdish *agha* (or 'chief') from the nearby mountains had been put in prison in Mardin. Unfortunately, the foundations proved too weak for the massive stone slabs, and when the house was nearly finished and its lower part occupied, they gave way, destroying part of the wall and causing the arches to fall. By the time repairs began the *agha* was out of prison and, feeling his local control of the population threatened, organised a determined opposition to the completion of the building. The rumour soon went round that it was a church rather than a house that was being built, and it took four years of battling with government bureaucracy and challenging the authority of successive *aghas* before it was finally completed.

The local population was impressed by this triumph of the 'Protestants' despite the heavy odds against them. Deciding that there must be considerable power behind them, the inhabitants soon came asking for instruction and for teachers for the out-lying villages.

It was not long before the Kurdish *aghas* in the surrounding mountains were at war with each other again and, for safety's sake, the helpers at Midyat had to retreat to Mardin for awhile. It was only after troops were sent in that some semblance of order was established in the area, and some of the more renegade *aghas* were either executed or banished forever from the region. A missionary called Miss Sears wrote from Midyat on 17 February, 1881, remarking that the head of one of the rebel chiefs, called Hajoo, was being displayed there on a tall pole for the interested crowds on that Sunday afternoon, and contrasted this 'barbarous entertainment' with the 'quiet assembling of the Protestant congregation' – for a small church had already sprung into being since the new house had been completed.

The house that one day was to be the home of Kenan Araz was used for thirty-six years as a centre of evangelical life and witness for the whole area round Midyat. Isaiah himself never lived to see the strange series of events that would one day take place beneath the arches he had toiled to build and then re-build. But already in the 1870s the Ottoman Empire was steadily moving closer to an abyss that would prove final and fatal, and the strange and terrifying events that would one day take place in Midyat were to form but a tiny part of the death throes of an Empire.

2
Revival and Massacre

For the Christians of the Ottoman Empire, the turn of the century was marked by the fires of revival as well as by the very different fires of massacre. Both left an indelible mark upon the Christian communities and, in a sense, Kenan Araz was destined to be a child of both.

As God purified the newly-founded churches, so thousands more were brought into the kingdom, and today the spiritual grandchildren of those new believers are to be found in every corner of the world. But, just as the church was expanding and beginning to make an impact upon the surrounding Muslim world, so whole communities and churches were sucked into eternity by a series of bloody massacres in which more than a million people lost their lives. A wedge was driven between the Christians and Muslims, a wedge of hatred and violence. A yawning chasm of fear and revenge was created that had never before existed on such a scale. It was a chasm that could only be crossed by the love and grace of God.

Despite Abdulhamid ...

To this day, the name of Sultan Abdulhamid has a special ring in Turkish ears, and if there is one point on which Turkish historians are united, it is that Abdulhamid's long reign from 1876 to 1909 was one of unrelieved despotism.

It was a time when Turkey was becoming increasingly known as 'the Sick Man of Europe'. In the year that Abdulhamid had come to power, a revolt had broken out in Bulgaria that had been put down with great ferocity by Ottoman irregular forces, an event which produced a strong reaction in the rest of Europe and led to pressure for reform.

With the rebellion of these Ottoman provinces in the west, and with Russia nibbling at the eastern borders, it seemed that the once mighty Ottoman Empire was ready to crumble. In a desperate attempt to hold onto the reins of power and keep his Empire together, Abdulhamid tried to centralise greater authority in his sultanate. Helped by the newly-installed telegraphic system and a vast network of spies, the Sultan became a professional eavesdropper on his Empire, paranoiacly watching for signs of criticism and discontent.

It was against this backcloth of increasing repression that the evangelical Church of Turkey grew so rapidly during the closing years of the nineteenth century. The growth was largely in the traditional Christian communities. By 1911, amongst the Armenians alone there were 329 evangelical churches with more than 20,000 church members and 378 mission schools catering for thousands of students. National workers totalled 1,191 along with 200 missionaries. There was hardly a town or village in the Empire where the gospel could not be heard, at least occasionally.

Centering upon the churches in Marash and Gaziantep, the Spirit of revival began to flow out and touch the surrounding areas in ever-widening circles. Those from the churches in Marash began to visit neighbouring Mardin, and the church in Midyat too experienced years of revival during which earlier divisions were healed, many were converted, and the believers built a large imposing church with room for several hundred worshippers and a school above it.

One key factor in the revival was fearless biblical preaching by a gifted local leadership; by men such as Ibrahim Levonian of Gaziantep, whose father had been amongst the first to come to Christ when the gospel came to the city in the 1840s. Totally dedicated, tending towards an ascetic and somewhat legalistic lifestyle, but full of compassion for the lost, Levonian's preaching was influential throughout the whole area.

During the times of revival three meetings were held every evening, the third continuing until midnight or later, as the Spirit moved. Since the Christians made up a good proportion of the population in cities such as Gaziantep and Marash, the new revival songs were soon being sung in homes, schools and market places. Many Muslim Turks also attended the meetings. The revival was marked by public confession of sin and restitution of property; well-known church leaders were amongst those who put things right with people they had injured. It was one of those rare occasions in Turkish history when many Muslims were able to witness a Christian community in their midst demonstrating real New Testament life and love. Not surprisingly, many were touched. As Ibrahim Levonian once put it:

> 'The most important and pressing need of our age and time is unity and love. There is no substitute for brotherly love – nothing can take its place. Our need is not for eloquent preachers, but for preachers who live their sermons eloquently.'

In 1905 the Swedish missionary evangelist Fredrik Franson visited Turkey for a preaching tour. It was the same year that revival had broken out in Wales. For months before his arrival, groups of believers had been gathering to pray for the meetings. Franson had been much influenced by D L Moody, and had worked with him for some time in Chicago. A tall and imposing man with a large bushy beard, Franson's preaching was simple and biblical, full of parables and anecdotes. He came to Marash for one night, but ended up preaching every night for six solid weeks. People from every background – Protestant, Catholic, Gregorian and Muslim – packed the church, clinging onto the doors and windows so that they could hear the word of God. The church was crowded hours before the meeting was due to begin. Hundreds were converted as Franson preached on the need for repentance, the joy of obedience

to the will of God, the transience of human life and the
certainty of judgment to come.

Who could know then that within three years Franson
himself would be dead and twenty-seven of the local
believers massacred, and that within fifteen years the
church building would be a smouldering ruin, with a great
majority of the thousands who came to those meetings
either killed or scattered to other lands.

The Student Volunteer Movement

While leadership of the churches was largely in local
hands, missionaries still played a key role in pioneering
new areas and in Bible teaching and educational work. It
was an age in which missionary interest among western
churches was high. Many others beside Franson had been
challenged and trained by the ministry of D L Moody, and
the work of the Student Volunteer Movement was having
an impact all over the world, with a steady stream of
volunteers swelling the already sizeable missionary task
force hard at work throughout the Ottoman Empire.

A dramatic appeal for reinforcements was sent to the
hundreds of students gathered for the International
Student Missionary Conference held in London in the first
few days of 1900. The appeal was signed by twelve former
leaders of British university Christian Unions already
serving abroad, Temple Gairdner of Cairo and Douglas
Thornton being amongst the signatories:

> 'Fellow students, we plead with you to speedily send
> reinforcements that the conquest of the world, which
> our great Captain is surely achieving, may be brought
> nearer and his Kingdom of Love established among
> men .... Will you hesitate to invest your life where it
> will count most for the Kingdom of God, and for the
> evangelisation of the world in this generation? We are
> solemnised as we ponder the profound issues which
> may flow from your decisions. Their influence will

extend far beyond your own lives, affecting the destinies of thousands, even millions of your fellow men.'

At the same conference Robert Speer challenged the delegates about the needs of the Ottoman Empire:

'Turkey is a hard field. There is no harder mission in this world than there, but there has never been a time when so clearly as today the voice of God was calling men to undertake the task. Men have died for carrying Christ to the South Sea Islands. Men have died for carrying Christ to China. Why should men be unwilling to die for carrying Christ also to the Muslims in the Turkish Empire?'

There were many who responded. By 1914, some 2,098 members of the British section of the Student Volunteer Movement alone had gone overseas. Many were destined to fulfill Speer's challenge to the letter, and died serving the people they were seeking to reach.

Inward-looking analysis of the rightness or otherwise of the missionary cause was not a characteristic of the age. Many who went out were rugged individualists, often brilliant academically or in sport, and not afraid to invest their lives where they would 'count most for the Kingdom of God'.

In the Ottoman Empire the missionaries were held in wide respect by Christian and Muslim alike as people of principle who were quick to help any community in need. They did not easily give up. Alpheus Andrus ran the mission station in Mardin for forty-five years. When his wife died only six years after they went to Turkey, he returned to America for a short break together with the only other missionary then working in Mardin, one Miss Parmelee. Undeterred, they returned to Mardin the following year as husband and wife.

The gathering clouds

There is little doubt that many Muslim Turks heard the
gospel during this era through the combined efforts of
missionary witness, the clearly visible church fellowships
in some areas, and the sale of scriptures by the Bible
Society. Yet the great majority of Muslims remained
outside these influences, for a number of reasons.

For centuries the Ottoman Empire had existed as a loose
conglomeration of separate peoples. The Muslim Turks
were the administrators and fighters – two noble tasks that
marked them out as the conquerors of the area. The
conquered Christian races were allowed to carry on their
lives in relative peace, pursuing less influential enterprises
such as trade and commerce. Each community had its own
language and courts and, increasingly during the
nineteenth century, its own western protector state to step
in and stand up for its rights during times of oppression.

It was therefore quite possible for Christians to live in a
community and have minimal contact with Muslims,
particularly in those many villages where the populations
were not mixed. Even in big cities like Istanbul, where in
1900 the population was only fifty per cent Muslim (the
remainder of the city being either Christian or Jewish),
each community lived in its own particular area.

Since the government oppression in the 1860s and 1870s,
following a brief period when many Turkish Muslims came
to Christ, there had been little systematic attempt to
evangelise Muslims. The aim of most of the missions was to
revive the historic churches in the area so that they
themselves would reach the large Turkish Muslim
majority. But this 'quantum leap' in outreach never really
took place. Only the most zealous believers from a
Christian background witnessed much to Turks, and the
social and linguistic differences tended to seal the
particular communities into their own cultural worlds. If a
Muslim did come to Christ, the reaction from his family and
community was often so drastic that the whole local
Christian minority would suffer, leading to pleas from

more 'balanced' church leaders to leave Muslim evangelism well alone.

A new and ominous factor was created during the nineteenth century by the gradual break-up of the Ottoman Empire and consequent increase in nationalistic aspirations amongst its nominally Christian subject peoples. Greece won her independence as a result of the war of 1826, and it was not unnatural that the Greeks still living within the boundaries of the Empire should begin to dream again of a restored Byzantium. The Armenians also began to hanker increasingly after self-rule.

The situation of the Assyrians was rather different. They lived in a relatively poor part of the Empire. Small in number, they posed little political threat, and had no historical nation of their own that they could claim had one day in the past been 'wrested' from them by the Turks. Their very name came from their church affiliation, not from their race – a fine point of distinction not always understood by the Turks.

However, the attitude of many of the more politically-orientated Armenians became increasingly nationalistic. While most Armenians steered clear of politics, a minority became involved in secret opposition plots against Sultan Abdulhamid. In 1894 the Sultan's opportunity came to strike back. The Armenians of the mountain district of Sassoun refused to pay their taxes, having recently been robbed by Kurds. The army was sent in to put down the rebellion. During the next two years 100,000 Armenians were massacred in different parts of the Empire, of whom some 10,000 were Protestants. About 100,000 widows and orphans were left by the massacres, and the churches and missionaries were busy in relief work for years after. Twenty-five Protestant pastors and 175 Gregorian priests lost their lives.

It is hardly surprising that the crushing of Abdulhamid's power in 1908 by a group of army officers was greeted with such relief. The Turks and Armenians embraced each other in the streets. An Armenian Bible Society colporteur in the

southern coastal city of Adana remembers marching up
and down the streets of the city, arm in arm with Muslim
Turks, shouting, 'Sultan Hamid is fallen! Sultan Hamid is
fallen! Liberty and justice for all!'

The group of army officers who broke the power of
Abdulhamid were known as the 'Young Turks'. Their
political expression was through the Committee of Union
and Progress and they had two main aims – the
preservation and renewal of the Empire, and the reform of
the constitution. Their driving force was Turkish
nationalism. No longer were they merely Ottomans,
content with a loose conglomeration of races in an Empire
which was rapidly falling apart. They were Young Turks,
disgusted by the incompetence of a decaying
administration and with their roots in the secular ideals of
the French Revolution, the positivist philosphy of Auguste
Compte, and the heady wine of the patriotic nationalism of
Turkish reformers such as Namik Kemal.

For the first time in an Islamic state the full force of that
western and essentially non-Islamic concept – patriotism –
was allowed full play. The power of the Sultan was broken
in 1908 and he was deposed by force in 1909. In the ensuing
confusion the message went out that the Sheriat, the Holy
Islamic Law, was threatened; in 1909 there was another
large massacre of Armenians, especially in Adana where at
least 20,000 lost their lives. This was all the more tragic in
view of the wave of optimism that had greeted the breaking
of the power of Abdulhamid only a year before.

It was just at this time that a convention of evangelical
church leaders was scheduled to be held in Adana. Twenty-
seven key local church leaders from Marash, Gaziantep
and the surrounding area set out for the conference. They
never arrived. On the way they spent a night in Osmaniye,
assembling in the church for a night of prayer. Unknown to
them the Adana massacre had already begun. Suddenly an
angry mob surrounded the church, quickly drenching it
with paraffin and oil. A match was applied – no one
escaped from the blazing inferno. The churches back in

Marash and Gaziantep never fully recovered from this devastating loss of leadership.

The storm breaks

Political theorists who are not themselves in power enjoy the luxury of building castles of idealistic policies in the air. Actual power brings with it responsibility, and with responsiblity comes reality. The Young Turks set out to renew the Empire through freedom and fraternity, with 'no distinction of race or creed', but in reality chose to accomplish the task through the incompatible policy of a vigorous Turkish nationalism. The whole concept of different *millets* became anathema.

Laws were soon passed banning any associations bearing the name of ethnic groups. The Turkish language was declared the exclusive medium of official business in the Empire. Non-Muslims were conscripted into the army. The Young Turks, being militant and efficient, put down all opposition with a ruthlessness that quickly surpassed that of Abdulhamid.

After some internal struggles a 'triumvirate' of *pashas* came to power and ruled by military dictatorship. Enver Pasha became Minister of War; Jemal Pasha, Military Governor of Istanbul; and Talat Pasha, Minister of the Interior.

It was during the upheavals of the First World War that the Young Turks saw their opportunity to solve once and for all the problem of the *millets*. In early 1915 a secret government decree was issued ordering the deportation of Armenians. This systematic plan began in early April in the Armenian mountain stronghold of Zeitoun. Some of the Armenians fought back but were overwhelmed; a great majority were simply deported. So began a pattern that was to be repeated again and again during the coming months, spreading like a dark red stain from east to west.

A deportation usually began with a public crier going through the streets announcing that every male Armenian

must present himself immediately at the Government
Building. The men would assemble in their working
clothes, leaving their shops open, their ploughs in the field,
their cattle on the mountainside. When they arrived, they
were thrown into prison, and then marched out of the town
in batches along some southerly road. They were starting,
they were told, on a long journey (to Mosul or perhaps to
Baghdad?). Like the Palestinians when forced from their
homes, many carried their house keys with them,
expecting soon to return. The vast majority never returned.
At the first lonely spot on the road they were halted and
massacred. Those who were not killed at this stage
struggled on. The survivors finally collected in deportation
camps in the south, before being sent to places like Aleppo
and Der-el-Zor in the Syrian Desert.

After the men had been deported, there was generally a
short respite, and then the women and children were
deported by the same route, being given a few days to wind
up their affairs. For them there was one escape route –
instant conversion to Islam. In some places whole villages
converted to escape deportation, and remain Islamic to
this day. For many believers it was a test by fire – either to
renounce their faith or set out on a road that might lead to
sudden death. Most stood firm. Probably more believers
were massacred in Turkey in 1915 than in any other year in
any other country so far this century, with the possible
exception of Uganda in the 1970s.

The details are gory, and there is little need to dwell on
them here. The story has been told often before. Those
deported from the east were sent by foot, those in the west
were deported by train in cattle trucks. Those on foot
perhaps suffered the most as they were left unprotected
from rape, pillage and murder by local bands of brigands.
Every day the straggling convoys would dwindle, and a trail
of rotting corpses marked the roads that they had been
forced to take. Rivers were favourite spots for killings. The
Tigris and Euphrates became choked with swollen and
mutilated bodies, drifting down towards the Syrian desert.

On 10 June, 1915, the German Consul of Mosul telegraphed that 614 Armenian men, women and children had been sent down the Tigris by raft from Diyarbakir – empty rafts had arrived at Mosul. Women gave birth on the road, but the babies rarely survived. When parents were massacred, babies were either left to die or were killed immediately by cracking their heads on a rock. Yet in the midst of these horrors believers managed to maintain some kind of witness. When the Christians from a village near Gaziantep were deported they started a daily prayer meeting on the road. Their pastor was killed but his last word to them was, 'Keep up the prayer meeting!' For seven weeks on the march, they did just that.

The massacre of 1915 was not a spontaneous turning of one community upon another; it was an organised government programme. There were many cases where Muslim Turks tried to protect their Christian Armenian neighbours, though if caught the punishment for them was death. Communities that had lived side by side for centuries were suddenly wrenched apart. The government made sure that the gendarmes guarding the convoys were of the most fanatical sort. Many prisoners were let out of prison with the deliberate aim of being used for the massacres. Kurdish tribesmen were given virtual *carte blanche* to attack the long columns of refugees. In some cases, such as at Van and Urfa, the Armenians were well armed and fought back, but in most cases they were simply led off like sheep.

Though the massacres were government sponsored, there were also cases where local Turks were only too glad to lend a helping hand. Sometimes there were old scores to settle. There were glittering prizes to be won – houses, fields and ploughs. Thousands of Turkish refugees had poured into Anatolia from both the crumbling eastern and western ends of the Empire, seeking new homes.

The missionaries were in the thick of it. For decades most of them had thrown in their lot with the Armenian community and did not forsake them in their hour of need.

However, in so doing they indelibly sealed in the minds of the Turks an impression that had been growing for years – that missionaries were agents of European intrigue, only existing by the protection of the western powers and were ultimately enemies of Turkey because they were working to strengthen the Christian minorities. A few missionaries were killed outright, but dozens died through accident and disease as they tried to minister to the immense needs around them.

The red stain steadily moved across the map. Cilicia was the first area to be cleared, with its large town of Adana. Then came Van and the strategic areas near the border immediately threatened by the Russian advance. In Bitlis, Mush, Sassoun and Hakkari there were no deportations, just wholesale slaughter on the spot. Like a heavy hand squeezing a tube, a whole race was either crushed where it was or forced inexorably down into the Syrian desert.

Some years later Talat Pasha, the Minister of the Interior, commented to a correspondent of the *Berliner Tageblatt*:

> 'The sad events that have occurred in Armenia have prevented my sleeping well at night. We have been reproached for making no distinction between the innocent Armenians and the guilty; but that was utterly impossible, in view of the fact that those who were innocent today might be guilty tomorrow . . . .'

Terror in Midyat

The new Protestant church building in Midyat had been opened in 1912. Many had come to Christ and the church was frequently packed. The Protestant community had become an integral part of the life of the town, and the new mission school and hospital served the whole surrounding area. Many of the church leaders were those who had been touched by years of revival. The help of the missionaries was much less needed than before. After forty years of hard work there was a flourishing indigenous church.

Down the road in Mardin things had been tough for some years. The old faithfuls were still there, but they were getting older and were not able to do so much. Dr Thom had already run the Mission Hospital for forty years. Alpheus and Parmelee Andrus were there too – by this time they had been working continuously in the area for forty-five years. Mrs Thom and Parmelee Andrus were both virtual invalids, and could only get about the mission station with the help of crutches. The disastrous winter and repeated plagues of locusts during the summer had caused great suffering, and once again the energies of missionaries and believers were directed into relief work.

Soon after the war broke out, both Alpheus Andrus and Dr Thom were deported by the authorities to Sivas, leaving their wives and four other single women to hold the fort in Mardin. Dr Thom died in Sivas. Soon afterwards Mrs Thom died, followed a few months later by Parmelee Andrus.

The life and example of these old and faithful missionaries had made an enormous impact on the believers of the area over the years. Year after year their lives could be read like open books. They were still foreigners, yet they truly belonged to the area in language, in custom and in their love for the people. It seemed natural that they should die in the land they loved. As the red stain reached Mardin and Midyat, it was clear that their example had not been in vain.

The Jacobite Assyrians were not intended as a prime target for deportation by the Young Turks. Their numbers were small compared to the Armenians, and their nationalistic aspirations very limited. But the government had not forgotten what had happened to their Nestorian Assyrian cousins in the mountains east of Midyat and in north-west Persia around Urmia. The murky theological history whereby one group of Assyrians were called Nestorians while the others were Jacobites was not something that interested the Young Turks. What was of more interest to them was that Urmia, a centre of Nestorian Assyrians, had been occupied by Russia in 1910. As war

broke out, the whole area found itself in the centre of the
conflict between Turkey and Russia. On the night of
Saturday 2 January, 1915, the Russians withdrew from
Urmia, and thousands of Assyrians fled with them towards
Russia. By the following morning the Christian villages of
the area were virtually deserted. Many of those who did not
flee were massacred. A few months later 35,000 Nestorians
from the mountains of Kurdistan were routed from their
homes by the Turkish Army; thousands were massacred
but many found safety behind the Russian lines.

Once again the message was being driven home –
Christianity was something that did not belong in the
Ottoman Empire; it was incompatible with Turkish
nationalism. The Christians fled behind enemy lines, and
not just any enemy, but the bitterest traditional foe of the
Turks – Russia.

Military efficiency dictated that the Jacobite Assyrians
around Mardin should not be left untouched, for the people
who were a security threat in one area might also be a
threat in some other place. Mardin was one of the main
towns on the deportation route to the south. The
inhabitants were well aware of what was going on to the
north and east of them. For months refugees had been
moving past the town, and the plain below was dotted with
the tents of temporary encampments. In July and August
Mardin's turn came. The pattern was as elsewhere, the
deportation and massacre of the town's Armenians and
many of the Assyrians – Catholics and Protestants –
being carried out with ruthless efficiency by the Governor
of the area.

Around the middle of July the government imprisoned
about a hundred leading Christian men of Midyat. Among
them were most of the leaders of the Protestant church;
men who had been built up in the word of God for many
years, men whose faith had become burning and fresh
through years of revival. They had seen God work. They
had seen their small town transformed since those early
days when the first missionaries had been stoned in the

streets – hundreds had come to Christ and the whole town had been touched at every level by the power of the gospel. For three years believers had been cramming for worship into the new solid stone church building, itself a witness to prayer, hard work and sacrificial giving.

Now these men were in prison. And the irony of it was that the prison was the very same building that Isaiah had laboured to build for the missionaries back in the 1870s. With the building of a new school and church buildings, it had no longer been necessary to keep the old house, so it had been sold as a local government building. The solid two-storey house with its cellar below remained, but an extensive courtyard had been added, with another much larger house at the end of it. The newer house was an imposing building built with the same large blocks of grey stone; two sizeable rooms formed the central government offices for Midyat, and beneath them ran a road through an archway. Since the large wooden gateway to the courtyard was also under the arch, this meant that visitors entering from either direction could be readily observed and vetted through the office windows above.

The cellar below the old missionary house made a very convenient prison as it had no windows, and its single door could be guarded easily because it led into the courtyard, surrounded by high walls. The prisoners in the cellar were surrounded by the arches that held up the house. They were the same arches that had collapsed and had had to be rebuilt by the believers who had sweated to build the house forty years earlier.

Being mid-July it was very hot. Without windows the prison was stifling as a hundred men were herded into a space designed to house a few cows. They were not all believers, but many were. Sometimes bands of relatives would make futile attemps to storm the building to release them, and they could hear the gunfire echoing up the narrow streets outside. The heavy stones of the archway over the road became pocked with bullet scars – scars that can be seen to this day. An attempt by other relatives to bribe the government to release the men also failed. They were accused of being spies. Why had they had so much contact with missionaries – foreigners who came from countries now at war with the Empire? Were they not a dangerous 'fifth column', just waiting for an opportunity to strike at the Empire like the wicked Armenians? All Christians must die.

There was every reason to be pessimistic. Every day news was reaching the town of the terror sweeping neighbouring areas. In Mardin the deportation had already begun. Though leaderless, the believers in Midyat who were still free spontaneously met daily for prayer in small groups, the wives and children of the imprisoned men lifting up their hearts to God for mercy upon their menfolk.

After a few days like this, one small girl could bear it no longer. She was just seven years old at the time. Inside the prison were her father, uncle and brother, together with many other relatives. Her father was the pastor of the church. Surely she could help them! Slipping away from home she raced down the narrow twisting cobbled streets of the town until she came to the large heavy door leading into the courtyard outside the cellar where the men were held. Her face streaming with tears, she beat on the door and pleaded: 'Please open it! I want to see my father!' Seeing the little girl in such distress, the soldiers took pity on her and let her in. Suddenly she felt sick with apprehension – what would she see inside the prison? The soldiers took her to the heavy padlocked door leading to the cellar. To her amazement the sound of cheerful hymn singing was filtering out from inside. Within a few seconds she was in her father's arms. The atmosphere in the prison was more like a revival meeting than a doomed men's cell! The impact of those few precious minutes made an impression on her that she would never forget.

It was the last time she ever saw her father, brother and other relatives. Just one week later they were bound to each other and marched out of the cell. Everyone knew what was going to happen next. Singing hymns, they

marched along the street leading out of the town with their
heads held high. Small groups of wives, families and friends
gathered on the flat roofs to see them go. Suddenly an
extraordinary sound echoed around the buildings. It was
the *kileli*, that distinctive high-pitched sound made at the
back of the throat by Assyrian women at times of great
rejoicing, such as weddings and the safe birth of a baby.
Someone had started the *kileli*, and it was quickly picked
up by the other watching women, many of whom were
seeing their husbands being led off to certain death.

That one high-pitched sound spoke more than a hundred
sermons. It meant that death had lost its sting. It meant that
decades of hard missionary labour had produced a harvest
of fruit that would remain – people who knew where they
belonged. The contrast with the wailing and weeping at the
usual Muslim and nominal Christian funerals of the area
could not have been more startling. As the men went, they
sang:

> 'We are going to be with Jesus.
> We do not fear death.
> Let them kill us, we are going to be with Jesus.
>
> They take away our clothes and leave us naked.
> They beat us so much, we cannot sleep at night.
> We had to sleep in a dark room, but we praise the Lord.
>
> They cut off our heads with an axe, we are going to be with
> Jesus.'

For six hours they were marched along, until they came
to a clearing surrounding a large hole in the ground that
served as a well. There they were gunned down by the
soldiers and their bodies were thrown down the well.

Back in Midyat the families of the men were placed
under house arrest. Tension in the village was high. There
was wide expectation that a more general massacre was to
follow. Gradually threatened families were smuggled out

of the town at night. Within a few weeks most of the Christian population of Midyat had escaped to a small village called Einwert situated on a hill-top about seven miles away. Rapidly this village of a few hundred people grew to a population of 6,000. Among those who escaped were the grandparents, great aunts and great uncles of Kenan Araz, all of whom were small children at the time.

In Midyat the fury broke. Any Christians remaining in the town, whether Protestant or Jacobite, were either massacred or forced, on pain of death, to become Muslims. Many children were taken off and forcibly 'adopted' into Muslim families in nearby villages.

It was soon discovered that most of the Christians in Midyat had slipped away to Einwert. The village was quickly surrounded by soldiers, who then proceeded to lay seige to it for the next three months. The conditions in the tiny village were appalling. Fortunately the people had taken their animals with them, but even so the food was scarcely enough. Worst of all was the chronic lack of water, as the water source lay the other side of the seige line. Many were shot as they tried to break through the lines at night to fetch water.

Every night the tiny church in Einwert was packed for times of prayer and worship. Completely cut off from the outside world, daily expecting to be massacred, many came to Christ at this time. In the lives of Kenan's grandparents spiritual fires were lit that would never be extinguished. Even the attacking soldiers seemed to realise that there were spiritual powers at work that all their guns could not overcome. To this day Muslims in the surrounding villages tell the story of how the soldiers, trying to shoot at the village at night, many times saw a figure in white walking on the roof of the church.

A government edict finally came ordering the seige to be lifted. The people of Midyat returned to their shattered town to find their houses ransacked, stripped of everything of value by the soldiers. There was hardly a family who had not lost a loved one. It was now mid October 1915, and winter was setting in. Many more died during the long cold winter as typhoid and other diseases swept the area. It took years for the shattered families to pick up the threads of their lives once again.

The aftermath of war

With the defeat of Germany in 1918 came also the break-up of the Ottoman Empire. For a while it seemed as if the area now known as Turkey would itself be fragmented. The Young Turk Triumvirate fled across the Black Sea on a German gunboat. An Allied fleet of sixty ships anchored in the port of Istanbul and the city was occupied. British forces took over the Dardanelles, Samsun, Gaziantep and other strategic cities. The French entered the area of Adana, and the Italians landed at Antalya. It seemed the 'Sick Man of Europe' was finally to die.

As the Allied forces moved in, so many of the Christians who had fled or been deported returned with them. Once again the same old message was imprinted upon the Turkish consciousness – Christianity was something that could only flourish under European armed protection, and was therefore alien to Turks and not rooted in the soil of Anatolia.

What happened in Urfa was typical of the places where the Allied forces moved in. The surviving Armenians from the city came up with the soldiers from the southern desert. Of the 5,000 homes that had been standing before the war, only a hundred were found intact when they returned. The old Protestant church bell was recovered from its hiding place, set up in the belfry, and rung by a young Armenian. The ancient church was soon packed with a thousand standing, and as the bell rang out the congregation fell into singing and sobbing. Similar scenes occurred as troops moved in to Gaziantep and the churches there were opened once again.

In May 1919, Greek troops landed in Izmir (Smyrna) under the protection of Allied war ships and began to

advance eastwards into Anatolia. This was too much for
the Turks. Four days later Mustafa Kemal Pasha, the
victorious Turkish hero of Gallipoli, landed in Samsun on
the Black Sea coast of Anatolia, and began to organise a
determined three-pronged opposition against the Greek
advance, the Allied forces of occupation, and the enfeebled
remnants of the Ottoman Government in Istanbul.

The Greek landing, and the treaty of Sèvres in 1920, by
which the Allied powers planned to carve up Turkey into
areas of western influence, were the two key events that
strengthened support for Mustafa Kemal and led directly to
the War of Independence. Once again Anatolia was the
scene of turmoil and bloodshed. This time French and
Armenians fought side by side against the nationalist
Turkish troops of Kemal. In the west the battle was
between 'Christian' Greeks and the Turks. In places, Turk
fought Turk as the nationalist forces clashed with
remnants of the Ottoman army.

It was the nationalist Turkish army under Mustafa Kemal
that eventually emerged victorious as French and
Armenians were pushed back from the south, as the
Greeks were literally driven into the sea at Izmir, and as the
war-weary Allies withdrew. The victorious Mustafa Kemal,
now better known as Ataturk (the 'father of the Turks'),
declared Turkey a Republic, and through a forceful
dictatorship set Turkey on a western and secularised
course.

Kemal Ataturk succeeded in doing in the 1920s what the
Shah of Iran later failed to do – break the political power of
Islam. The caliphate was abolished and Islam ceased to be
the official religion, the last hapless caliph being packed off
to Europe on the Orient Express. Turkey officially became
a secular state. European laws were introduced, the Latin
alphabet was enforced in place of the Arabic and the fez
was abolished in favour of the dreaded hat (which would
not allow the devout Muslim to touch his forehead to the
ground in prayer).

The question of the sizeable population of Christian

Greeks that remained was solved by a callously efficient method. In 1923 1.5 million Greeks from Turkey were exchanged with 400,000 Turks from Greece. Since more than 300,000 Greeks were evacuated from western Turkey at the close of the War of Independence, this meant that the new Turkish Republic was effectively depopulated of most of its Christian minorities. In this way, as part of one of the largest organised population exchanges in the world's history, thousands of Greek believers went to Greece, and hundreds more churches closed down in the north and west of the country.

Thus, the effects of a hundred years of missionary outreach were largely neutralised through the convulsions of the First World War and the Turkish War of Independence that followed it. Small pockets of believers remained, but they were now part of communities that had been largely stripped of their former power and influence and subdued by the terrible events that had been flooding over them for so many years. Some missionaries were allowed to remain, but only on the condition that they did not proselytise. For many this fitted well with their new concept of mission, as a seeping universalism had already taken its toll of evangelistic zeal, and educating a new generation of secularised Turks to follow the Christian principles of European civilisation fitted better with their concept of the kingdom of God than did the 'vulgar' concept of converting Muslims.

A new generation of believers was needed – believers who would have both the love and the courage to break out of the ghetto mentality of the minorities, and clothe the gospel in Turkish garb, such that Turks would see not the threatening tentacles of western Christian imperialism but the Christ who himself fell like a seed into the earth to die so that all men might have life.

3
On a Christian Island
in a Muslim Sea

Midyat, 1940

There was great rejoicing in the Araz family on 28 August, 1940, as their first-born came safely into the world. The fact that the baby was a boy was an extra cause for thankfulness, so they called him 'Amanuel'. Amanuel's father, Enver, was away in the army doing his military service at the time, but came hurrying back at the first opportunity to share in the family's joy.

What's in a name? In the Middle East it may mean everything. A name means identity, religion, community, roots. . . . For Amanuel his name immediately singled him out as a Christian Assyrian. No Turk would know that the name meant 'God with us', but every Turk would see the name 'Amanuel' as something strange and non-Turkish.

In the Midyat of 1940 this mattered little. After all, ninety per cent of the village's population was still nominally Christian, the remaining ten percent Muslim. Since the average family size was eight, the population had quickly recovered from the ravages of the war years. So the traditional Christian dominance of the town had remained, despite everything, and there were still plenty of 'Amanuel's' around.

Eighteen years later Amanuel was to change his name to a Turkish Muslim name, Kenan. So from now on he will be referred to simply as – 'Kenan'.

Kenan came into a family that was full of warmth and love. His grandfather, Yusuf, who had become a believer through attending the missionary college in Mardin during the time of Alpheus Andrus, had been a figure greatly loved and respected by the whole town. So deep was this trust that, during times of dispute between two families, each side would come to Yusuf for judgment rather than taking the case to court.

Yusuf's generation of believers and their parents were those who had experienced times of both great revival and bloody massacre. Most of this generation had lost their lives in 1915, including many of Kenan's great uncles. Much of the love and enthusiasm of those who survived had been passed on to the next generation but, sadly, without deep spiritual roots. After the war years, division on the one hand and apathy on the other began to stifle the witness and effectiveness of the local church. True, there was still a faithful remnant, and on special occasions the church would be packed as in the old days. But it was a post-revival generation, few of whom were themselves experiencing daily spiritual reality.

As the Protestant Church began to lose its evangelical cutting edge, so its very *raison d'être* was brought into question, leading to a drift back to the Jacobite Church by some, and an irrational pride in others of being Protestant without any clear idea of what this involved spiritually.

It was only in later life that Kenan's parents came into a more personal knowledge of God. At the beginning Kenan was part of a family that was sufficiently Protestant not to share in some of the more extreme superstitions common at the time, but not Protestant enough for the Bible to be read and practised, rather than simply being placed under the pillow at night as a kind of talisman. From an early age Kenan was sent to Sunday School in the church, where Abdul-Mesih Gonench was then pastor, a position he held for forty-four years. Mr and Mrs Araz did not generally go to church except for special occasions.

Kenan's father was a tubby and jovial figure, his large and jowly face readily breaking into a beaming smile. Like his father Yusuf before him, he was known for both his generosity and wisdom, though in his case the ability to solve disputes amicably became his profession, since he made a living as a lawyer once his military service was complete.

Kenan's mother was a small, wiry, hard-working woman with bright eyes and a quick infectious laugh. For her, as for Enver, Kenan was always special. After Kenan, she gave birth in quick succession to nine more children, of whom three died in childbirth, leaving Kenan eventually with five sisters and one brother. But nothing could replace the fact that Kenan was the first-born son.

The spiritual power-house of the family in those days was Kenan's grandmother. As the number of grandchildren grew, so she wept in prayer for each of them, as she did for their parents, that the next generations might share in her living personal faith.

The first language of the household was Syriac, the language of the Assyrians kept alive in its ancient form in the liturgies of the Jacobite Church, and in its spoken form in the daily lives of the people. The second language was Kurdish, spoken by most of the Assyrians in the area; its use was widespread due to the large population of the Kurds in the surrounding towns and villages. The third language was Arabic, reflecting the influence of neighbouring Syria and Iraq to the south, where so many Assyrians had moved during the break-up of the Ottoman Empire. Kenan soon learned to speak Arabic fluently, though he was never able to read or write it. The fourth language of the household was Turkish, for this was a language learned more in school and in the army than in the home. Most Assyrians spoke it with a strong accent that grated on the ears of Turks who might occasionally visit from faraway places such as Istanbul or Ankara.

What's in a language? In Turkey it is said truly that the number of languages you know determines the range of persons you can be. Every new language mastered means the potential to be another person, another character.

Language means identity, race, belonging. . . . Kenan grew up thinking in Syriac but speaking four languages altogether, each one representing different aspects of the tempestuous times through which the area had passed.

Which language – which personality – was ultimately going
to dominate his life still remained to be seen.

The house at Little Lake

Kenan's home was a rich and prosperous one by the
standards of the time. The Araz family was one of the
leading families of the town. As the only lawyer in the area
specialising in land disputes, Enver was much in demand,
and was a familiar figure as he travelled on horseback to
the dozens of villages around Midyat. Himself speaking
four languages, he had many Christian and Muslim friends,
rich and poor alike; and as they frequently visited the Araz
household, Kenan grew up learning how to relate to people
from very varied backgrounds.

Mr Araz was always ready to buy the latest thing for his
eldest son, and when Kenan was seven he was given a
brand new bicycle. It was the very first bicycle in the town
and became a source of envy for all the other children of
the area.

In 1949 Enver bought the old missionary house, together
with the larger government building that had been annexed
to it before the First World War. When the Araz family
moved it seemed to Kenan, then nine years old, as if they
were moving into a palace. The whole property was indeed
extensive. The original house built by Isaiah back in the
1870s still stood firm, though the prison where the church
leaders had been locked up in 1915 had long since been
converted into a stable and storehouse. The large open
courtyard now had two wells, extremely useful during the
long hot dry summers (running water was unheard of in the
area).

Outside stairs led up from the courtyard to a wooden
balcony that ran around one end of the courtyard at the
level of the main living quarters. These were furnished
richly, the deep reds of the large thick Turkish carpets
blending with the dark blues of the curtains and cushion
covers. The two large upper rooms, which had once been

the seat of government for the area, were reached by a corridor that passed through the archway above the road. One room was reserved for receiving guests. It had a cushioned ledge running around the wall to serve as a seat during the day and as a bed for extra guests if necessary. The other room served as a dining room when guests came, and on the walls were cabinets containing the best dining-ware, photographs and other bric-à-brac. Deep alcoves for the windows in both these rooms emphasised the massive thickness of the walls. The impression of living in a castle was heightened by the fact that the house was still on the very edge of Midyat, and the view from the windows looked directly across to the surrounding rolling hills.

The bullet scars on the outside walls were still clearly visible as a vivid reminder of all that had gone before, but the bullet marks on the ceilings of the two large guestrooms were there from different causes. During times of great rejoicing, such as wedding celebrations, it was customary for the men present to draw their revolvers and shoot at the ceiling, a practice that would be less advisable in Turkish houses of more recent date which are not always built of such durable materials.

The bedrooms of the Araz household were the other side of the archway and were in a style typical of the time, with some of the children sleeping in large alcoves set in the walls, and others on mattresses on the floor, or in actual beds. Underneath the mattress of the only double bed was a large loaded pistol. Security in the area has always been more a question of self-defence than one of waiting for the relevant security forces to arrive, and clashes and raids between villages in the area continue to the present day.

Being a rich house it boasted a telephone. This had a long black handle that required vigorous cranking to attract the attention of the operator. The number – Midyat 94 – reflects the rarity of telephones at the time.

Visitors would, of course, come unannounced and at all times of day and night, and were received with the warmth and hospitality that have always characterised households

of typical rural Anatolia. A visit would begin with heavy
hammering on the large wooden door under the archway.
This was the very same door on which the little girl had
knocked, asking to see her father in prison, all those years
before. The visitors would be welcomed in, the men
greeting the men with a kiss on both cheeks, and the
women kissing the women likewise. Muddy or dusty shoes
would be left at the door to be replaced by slippers. Then
men and older women would be ushered into the visitor's
room, while younger women would busy themselves in the
kitchen, or gather together in some other part of the house.
Other visitors might already be sitting on the ledge around
the edge of the visitor's room. As each new visitor came in,
so they would shake hands individually with every other
person in the room, with the exception of the elderly,
whose hand it was polite to take, kiss and then hold briefly
to one's forehead. Only then could the visitor take his seat,
and even then it was best to look for a seat that was less
comfortable or advantageous than the others so that the
host could force you to take a better place.

The men would sit rather stiffly without crossed legs, the
women frequently being more comfortable with their legs
drawn up beneath them, well-covered by voluminous
skirts. A haze of cigarette smoke would quickly settle
across the room and, if it was winter, a wood stove would
add its own contribution to the rather acrid atmosphere. As
the guests warmed up, so the conversation would become
more animated, especially if it had anything to do with land
disputes.

The hospitality given followed a set pattern. At the
beginning a younger member of the family would be
assigned to take a bottle of cologne around and sprinkle it
on the hands of the guests. Strong black Turkish coffee
would then be served on a copper tray, the loud sucking of
coffee through pursed lips being an expression of
appreciation. After a suitable pause – short if you wished
your guests to leave early, longer if you wished them to stay
– tea would be brought and served, without milk, in small

glasses. With it would come biscuits or cakes. The final step was the fruit, which could not be a mere lonely apple on a plate but had to be a large plateful for each person of several of the best fruit in season. When the fruit had been consumed, it was time to go. The manner of parting was as important as the coming. The right greetings had to be passed on, the right pressure applied to ensure that the guests would soon return for another visit. Finally they would be escorted to the gate and, if they were especially honoured, part-way down the road as well, before exchanging farewells.

As the privileged 'eldest son' (*ağabey*), Kenan was frequently present at these times and, sitting close to his father, would join in the warmth and spirit of the occasion. The enjoyment of people that he imbibed in this way never left him. It was the joy of community, both within the family household, often expanded to include all kinds of people, and within the town – the simple but profound joy so sadly ravaged by the pressure of urbanised societies. When Enver's brother and his wife were in sudden need of a home, they moved in with their six children to join the household. For the growing children of both families there was never a dull moment.

Stories

Every community in the Middle East lives to a certain extent in the past, drawing from stories passed down through the generations. In many places absence of a secular state and limited urbanisation has helped to preserve a sense of local historical continuity.

For Kenan, being brought up in Midyat as a Protestant meant that there were constant reminders of the bitter past. In the neighbouring house on one side lived an elderly woman whose parents had both been killed during the massacres of 1915, and who had then been brought up by missionaries in an orphanage. In the house on the other side was another family who had also lost many relatives at the same time.

Kenan picked up the stories of the past very quickly from listening to the older visitors as they sat around the stove reminiscing on cold winter evenings. Sometimes he would sit at the door of the storehouse below the old house at the end of the courtyard, and he would close his eyes and try and picture the scene as if the room was crowded with prisoners. With a little imagination, the wind whistling past the heavy stone blocks of the house could become the singing of a packed group of men and, with a slight shiver, Kenan would remember how many of his relatives had spent their last days on earth in that very place.

Yet, in the Araz household at least, the past was not recalled with acrimony. What was past was past, and there was little point in reviewing old horrors and stirring up revenge for a new generation. Other families were not so wise in their approach, and there was many an Assyrian family in which the object-lessons of the past were dragged out to make sure that the spirit of hatred for Muslims in general – Turks and Kurds in particular – was effectively passed on to the new generation. The job of sowing hatred was made much easier by the frequent fights and raids between nominal Christian and Muslim villages during which Christians certainly gave as good as they got.

Kenan's grandmother was a great source of stories about the past, and on long winter evenings would sit with Kenan around the stove, regaling him with tales of massacre and persecution – of the heroes of faith of past generations who had preferred death to renouncing their faith.

One man always stood out in Kenan's mind above all the rest because of his love and his irrepressible faith, and the way that he refused to be cowered by opposition. The man's name was Haralambos Bostancioğlu and Kenan never tired of hearing his story.

Haralambos was a Greek who had been brought up in Adana. After graduating from St Paul's College in Tarsus in

1906, he had one unswerving ambition – to become an evangelist in his native city of Adana. For some years he worked with a large evangelical church that was active in Tarsus at that time. Later he moved to help a mission orphanage near Kayseri. There he met and married Aneta, one of the teachers. His courtship with Aneta was characteristically blunt. In one letter he wrote:

> 'My love for you is always fresh, and if I ever marry, you are the only one I want. But remember that I am a person spurned and despised. You won't be sharing any popularity or notability. You can only expect suffering in your lot with me. My life and my preaching will someday lead me to an unnatural death. Should you be willing to commit your life to such a husband, let us continue writing to each other.'

Haralambos was weak in tact and strong in faithfulness. He gave up his job at the orphanage to become an itinerant evangelist, and soon became well-known in the churches of Anatolia, his ministry being felt far beyond his original goal of Adana. After preaching in the churches at Gaziantep for awhile, he was banned from several pulpits as his messages were apparently a little too direct. Undeterred, Haralambos was given the keys of an old disused Anglican church by a sympathetic British missionary, and the large derelict building was soon crowded with people. After a short imprisonment and the traditional beating of the feet with a stick (on false charges), Haralambos finally moved on.

On another occasion he teamed up with a Bible Society colporteur, Stylianos, who was active in Adana. Stylianos was a short loud-voiced man who wrote long poems about the Bible in Turkish, which he would read in public places before selling the Scriptures. During one trip Haralambos and Stylianos loaded the horse-cart with Bibles and set out on the dusty track leading along the southern Mediterranean coast to Silifke. Wherever they stopped both would sing hymns in public places, after which

Stylianos would recite his flowing poems while Haralambos played his violin, an approach which would not go down very well in today's Turkey, but which at the time attracted large and sympathetic crowds of Muslims who apparently bought great quantities of Bibles.

In 1914 Haralambos was back in Gaziantep, again holding meetings in the old Anglican church, which once more was packed with people every evening. Liberal theology had been creeping into the local churches for some time. Determined to put things to right, Haralambos set up his own printing press and started a magazine called *The Truth*. A choir and Bible school were also soon organised, and then a primary school.

The local ecclesiastical authorities felt threatened by this success, and the opposition began. It was soon after this, in August 1915, that deportation of the city's Armenians began. Since Haralambos was a Greek, it seemed unlikely that he would be included in the deportation and the meetings were continued, though the numbers dwindled as more and more were deported. Then, one Friday evening that month, policemen came to his home, ransacked it, and arrested him, leaving Aneta alone in a strange city.

Who would take the service that Sunday? The bells were rung as usual half an hour before the service. Had the pastor been released? Everyone rushed to the church and there was soon a capacity congregation expectantly waiting. But Haralambos did not appear. Instead, Aneta calmly took her place in the pulpit. Aged 20, in the midst of conservative Muslim Gaziantep, in an Anglican church, she preached a powerful sermon on the lordship of Christ. As she concluded, a man was heard to murmur: 'In this couple there is a male lion and a female lioness!'

So the services continued until, six weeks later, all churches in Gaziatep were closed by government order. Haralambos was kept in prison. What made the separation even harder for Aneta to bear was the knowledge that he was being kept there through the malice of a high-ranking nominal Christian in the city who hated his preaching of the gospel.

Haralambos was then taken off in handcuffs to Urfa, a city about a hundred miles to the east on the way to Mardin. There a judge offered to free him on receipt of a suitable bribe, a common saying at the time being 'Ruşvet yemeden iş yûrûmez' ('Without a bribe nothing goes forward'). Haralambos refused and was sent back to Gaziantep, the judge unable to decide on a sentence. When the prison director saw him back with no sentence he wept, saying: 'This man is a saint; hardly anyone returns alive from Urfa!'

The prison director was a Turkish Muslim, a good man who was longing for Haralambos's release. His special delight was to listen to Haralambos playing the violin. On one occasion the director allowed him to return home for just one night, taking him there in person, on condition that he return to the prison early the next morning. Haralambos agreed and arrived on the doorstep, his clothes crawling with vermin, to greet a shocked Aneta. After his first bath for six weeks, and a short but joyful night at home, Haralambos was soon back in prison.

A whole year passed and still Haralambos was not sentenced. One morning Aneta was walking to the prison when whe saw a man dangling from the gallows in the main square – not an uncommon sight in the Gaziantep of those days. A sudden stab of fear went through her heart – 'My husband!' An elderly man noticed her alarm and approached her: 'Don't fear, my daughter. This is a soldier who was a deserter, a Muslim.' Slowly she raised her eyes to look. It was true; it was not Haralambos. But Aneta found she was trembling uncontrollably. At the prison Haralambos was full of the joy of the Lord, but in Aneta something had snapped. For the next few months, while the long uncertain weeks of imprisonment dragged on, Aneta suffered what she only later realised was a nervous breakdown. For two months she could not even face visiting Haralambos in prison. One day early in November 1916, she was crying out to God in prayer at a time of

darkest desperation, when suddenly the burden lifted and a
sense of peace returned. She immediately ran to the prison,
and a few days of joyful visits with Haralambos followed,
before the ominous news came that he was being sent off
to Marash.

It was 13 November 1916. Haralambos was in chains,
ready for the walk to Marash, just fifty miles away; this
journey ordinarily took two days but in chains it would
take three. When Aneta came to the prison that morning
and threw herself into his arms, for the first time through
all their trials she saw Haralambos cry, and next to him the
kind-hearted prison director wept as they said their final
farewells.

Aneta never saw her husband again. Later on she was
able to piece together the story of what happened at
Marash. By this time the city had been almost entirely
emptied of Christians. The churches that had once been
packed for revival meetings now lay empty and deserted.
Only a few German missionaries and a handful of local
believers remained. For a few weeks they were able to visit
Haralambos in prison and were witnesses to what finally
happened.

It was a bright morning in early December when
Haralambos was led out of his cell with sixteen others. The
small group, chained together, did not attract much
attention as they were led through the quiet streets of
Marash. Such great numbers had already been led off for
deportation that a mere seventeen was nothing special. But
in the main square, where the executioner went about his
task with professional skill, a sizeable crowd had gathered.
The loop of rope was in turn slipped over the head of each
condemned man while he stood on a chair dressed in a
white sleeveless robe with a label hanging from his neck
proclaiming his offence. Then, moving back a few steps,
the executioner ran forward with force, pushing the person
into the air away from the chair. With a quick grab, he
retrieved the chair for the next victim. Haralambos was
kept until last, so had the added torture of witnessing the

other sixteen die. When his turn came the label 'revolutionary' was placed around his neck, though the only 'revolution' he had ever preached was that of lives turned upside down through the love of Christ.

Calmly Haralambos, aged 32, climbed onto the chair, and in a quiet voice asked for permission to speak. The last request of the condemned was invariably granted. The crowd of silent onlookers pressed in to hear what this man of God would say:

'I praise my Lord for this day, because I have been allowed to suffer for his glorious name. You are sending me to my heavenly Father by the short route, though it has been an arduous experience. I am a preacher of the gospel and have nothing to do with the offence that is tagged on me'.

He then bowed his head and prayed his last prayer: 'Father, forgive them, for they know not what they do.'

The man in charge of the gallows approached him, placed the loop around his neck, and proceeded with the execution. Haralambos went to be with his Lord 'by the short route'.

The crowd watched in deep awe. It was a peculiar climax to this horrifying sequence of hangings. They could never have imagined that the last person to be executed would give them such thoughts on which to ponder. A German soldier stood nearby. With paper and pencil, he was making sketches. He remarked later on the extraordinary serenity with which Haralambos left this world.

Among the onlookers was a Muslim Turkish officer of high rank. He began thinking on the brief message he had heard. How could this man die so serenely? There was nothing in *his* religion that took the sting out of death in such a way. Compelled to know the source of the condemned man's faith, the officer approached a German soldier who was able to provide him with a Turkish Bible. This high-ranking Muslim officer subsequently found Christ.

When Kenan's grandmother finished the story of
Haralambos, she would turn to Kenan and remind him:

'Never forget that love is stronger than hate. Don't waste
your time hating Muslims! Jesus loves them – you love
them too. But you will never do it without God's power! It is
impossible by ourselves . . . .'

So something flowed from the life and death of
Haralambos Bostancioglu, just as it flowed from the life
and death of those massacred believers in Midyat, which
made a deep impact on Kenan. It was the message that
forgiveness is more revolutionary than retaliation – that
out of a seed falling into the ground comes life. It was the
message that the way of revenge is sterile and that the
Turkish church of the future was not to be reborn out of
recrimination, but through the way of reconciliation. It was
the message that the way to the Muslim heart was not
through confrontation, but through incarnation.

There was one part of the story of Haralambos that
Kenan's grandmother did not know. Two weeks after
Haralambos was executed, Aneta received a small piece of
leather. In it was hidden a four-page letter, written by her
husband just before he had been led out to die. The letter
was full of encouragement, full of joy, and full of the deep
assurance that the Lord would raise up other labourers
who would one day carry on. Aneta treasured this letter for
fifty-four years until finally in August 1970 she tore it up,
her eyesight too weak to read it any longer. Destroying it
was a traumatic experience, almost like burying
Haralambos anew, but by that time the assurance of the
letter had been amply fulfilled – other labourers were
carrying on.

Midyat and Estel

If anything symbolised the confrontation between Islam
and Christianity in the area of Midyat, it was the existence

of the town of Estel. Estel was the response of the new
nationalistic Turkish Republic to the existence of Midyat, a
town renowned for its high proportion of Christians and its
antipathy to all forms of central government. Estel was
established as the centre of government for the area. From
the start it was completely Muslim. No Christian family
would dream of living in Estel. Though on paper it was part
of Midyat, in practice it developed two miles away down a
straight treeless road that led across open countryside.

Estel reflected both the strengths and the weaknesses of
the new Republic. The government buildings were drab,
grey and functional, a pale reflection of the much larger
and equally characterless buildings that were erected at
the same time in the new capital city of Ankara during the
1920s and 1930s.

In Estel, growing up at the same time as Kenan, was
another young boy, but his family was strongly Muslim.
One day this boy would grow up, come to Christ, and be
one of the translators of the New Testament into modern
Turkish – but that day was as yet a long way off.

Down the road from Estel, Midyat was a town belonging
to another world: narrow, winding, muddy streets; high
stone walls and glimpses through open doors into
courtyards; church towers and ancient graveyards; tracks
that disappeared into the packed mud roofs of houses;
cattle and sheep jostling for position as they picked their
way along the narrow streets. No one could say that Midyat
was modern or efficient, but it had character and roots in
the area, its churches and monasteries dating back more
than fifteen centuries.

Somehow Enver Araz managed to encompass both
worlds – the world of Estel and the world of Midyat. He was
one of the few Christians who could regularly be seen
riding his horse down to Estel on business. Of course part
of the reason was purely commercial; there was a need for
a land lawyer at both ends of the road. But there was
something more than that. Kenan's father had the kind of
bigness of heart that could include both worlds, that was

willing to go out to people and take risks, and not just
huddle in an inward-looking community that felt itself
threatened by the encompassing sea of Islam

Mar-Gabriel

If Estel and Midyat symbolised the confrontation between
Islam and Christianity in the area, then the ancient
monastery of Mar-Gabriel (Deyr-ul-Umur) represented
withdrawal and renunciation. Set in desolate rolling hills
eleven miles from Midyat, its massive stone walls reflected
the fortress spirit of the faith that had built them.

No child from an Assyrian family could possibly forget
their first visit to Mar-Gabriel. The monastery, founded in
396 AD, was approached by a winding track that led to a
large, studded wooden door. As it swung open for the
visitors, a large courtyard was revealed, leading to another
gateway and a further jumble of buildings beyond, each
one reflecting the style of the century in which it had been
built. Standing out from its surroundings was the great
church built by Emperor Anastasis in 512 AD; its dome was
supported by walls several metres thick and the cold stone
slabs of its floor were worn by the passage of countless
worshippers over the centuries. From the semi-gloom of
the church, lit by a series of flickering candles that cast
dancing shadows over the walls, a passage-way led
downwards to underground rooms, cut out of solid rock,
where once monks had passed months in solitude in an
effort to grow closer to God. It was from these
underground cells that some had come to a new freedom in
Christ as the influence of the Bible had become
increasingly apparent during the previous century.

Jacobite, Catholic or Protestant, no Assyrian could
forget that Mar-Gabriel was already a well-established
centre of Christianity while the Turks were but a group of
nomadic tribes in central Asia, with many centuries yet to
pass before they even heard of Islam. The cultural and
religious roots of the Assyrians were here, and whatever

theology one professed, the life of the monastery with its ancient liturgies and withdrawal from the world was always seen as the religious ideal that ran as a common thread across denominational boundaries. It therefore seemed natural that even Assyrian families of a Protestant background should actively support the monastery, and in later life Enver Araz became the chairman of its Board of Trustees, a board legally required by the Turkish government's Law of Religious Foundations.

For the young Kenan, outings to the monastery were fun. Boys at the monastery school were his friends and together they would explore the hidden passage-ways and underground vaults. Meals were eaten together in the ancient dining-hall, occasions when the enforced silence was broken only by the rattle of tin cups on the long low stone tables.

Yet there was something about the spirit of the monastery that Kenan never absorbed and that never attracted him. It was the idea that religion is something morbid and introspective, that being religious means withdrawal rather than avowal. The biblical roots of Kenan's family, tested by fire in previous generations, had left a mark that made him different. For the rest of his life Kenan was to find himself, in personality and later in faith as well, clashing with the dominant monastic ideal of the Assyrian community as it presented itself in various forms and guises.

4

The Road to Istanbul

Kenan's early school days in Midyat passed quickly and uneventfully. Children of his age growing up in Midyat never saw buses, trains or planes. A trip down the road to Mardin was a major event and most older people passed their lives in Midyat and its vicinity, seeing no need to venture further afield.

For many of the new generation the atmosphere was stifling. Apart from working in the fields there seemed little else to do. The increasing number of radios brought news of life in far-off cities such as Ankara and Istanbul. More people were now able to read Turkish and the occasional Turkish newspaper would find its way to Midyat. All these factors contributed to a sense of restlessness.

There were two jobs at which people from Midyat had become very gifted – one was tailoring and the other was dealing in gold and precious stones. There was clearly a limit to the number of people who could be absorbed into these occupations in the Mardin area, and a steady trickle of families moved from Midyat to Istanbul where they set up business in and around the famous 'Covered Bazaar'. As the Assyrian community in Istanbul grew, so more and more people were drawn there by news of the good economic prospects and other attractions of city life.

In the summer of 1957 Kenan completed his primary education in the middle school of Midyat. Mr Araz was in a quandary. The nearest *lycée* for secondary education was in Mardin, but it had a bad reputation for being a rough school and his ambitions for his eldest son were set high. Kenan's sisters would be happy with a good but limited education, and a strong home life in which they would be trained for their future roles as housewives. But an eldest son . . . that was different.

Enver Araz's decision for Kenan was characteristically bold – he would be sent to boarding school in Istanbul, and not just any boarding school, but the famous Istanbul Boys' Lycée from which many well-known Turkish politicians, artists and businessmen had graduated. Kenan's mother was horrified at the thought of her only son having to live so far from the care and protection of home, but her objections were soon overruled. Thus, in September 1957, Kenan found himself in a heavily-laden *dolmush* (or 'shared taxi') bouncing down the road to Mardin, a large crowd of relatives and friends waving goodbye at the outskirts of the village until the vehicle pulled over the brow of the hill on the dusty road and could be seen no more. For the Araz family it was a moment of both pride and pain: pride in the thought that Kenan was the very first boy from Midyat to be sent off to boarding school in Istanbul, and pain at the wrenching apart of such a close family. It was perhaps just as well that they did not know then that Kenan was never again to live permanently in Midyat.

The journey

For Kenan the long journey to Istanbul was filled with both joy and trepidation. It was like travelling to a new world; indeed for him it *was* a new world. However, travelling across the length of Anatolia was not just a journey into the future but a journey into the past as well; every stopping place evoked its own special stories and memories.

All the way to Mardin the familiar banter and chatter continued in Syriac and Kurdish. September was the driest time of the year and a dusty haze hung over the fields, which had been harvested three months before. In Mardin there was hustle and bustle – Arabic now the predominant language – as friends helped Kenan in the transfer to the bus that would take him westward to Adana. With a shudder the old bus set off, and was soon rattling down the winding road that led out of the town towards the plain below. As Kenan looked back he could see the domes of the mosques, the towers of the churches and the arches and walls of houses seemingly packed against the hillside in a mosaic of grey stone. A verse wandered into his mind from Sunday School days: 'A city set on a hill cannot be hid.'

The bus journey to Adana took twelve hours. The road was full of pot-holes and the bus lurched and jolted as it swung from one side of the road to the other in a vain attempt to avoid the worst of the cavities. Painted across the front of the bus was the word *Mashallah*, intended to ward off the evil eye and prevent an accident. Two drivers handled the trip and exchanged places while the bus was in motion with professional nonchalance.

The stop on Urfa was a welcome break. As he got out of the bus to stretch his legs, Kenan could not help a slight shiver, remembering all the stories he had heard of what had happened to the Christians of Urfa. The bus stopped in a large parking area overlooking the older part of the town. Kenan did not know it, but as he looked across the fields during that brief stop he was looking towards the old monastery from where imprisoned missionaries during the first World War had watched the battle between Turks and Armenians. Nothing was left now of the church in Urfa.

A few hours later the bus stopped in Gaziantep, the town where years earlier men like Ibrahim Levonian and Haralambos Bostancioğlu had preached the word of God so faithfully; the town where churches had been packed for meetings for weeks on end, and where Muslims had come to Christ. As they went on to Adana, the bus passed through Osmaniye where those twenty-seven church leaders had been burned to death in the church as they gathered for a night of prayer back in 1909.

Then came Adana itself, a large bustling town on the rich Chukurova plain, now almost completely Turkish and strongly Muslim. Here also nothing remained of the strong evangelical fellowship of years past. Though Arabic could be heard in the streets, Turkish was by now the dominant

language, and Kenan began to feel relieved that he had
worked hard at his Turkish at school, unlike so many of his
friends who had thought it a waste of effort.

It was still a further twenty hours to Istanbul. The bus
this time was a very modern affair, as befitted such a well-
travelled route. As they left Adana, Kenan saw his very first
train, a splendid iron monster throwing out sparks and
clouds of steam as it pulled out of the station, bound for
Baghdad. Soon the bus turned off the coastal road at
Tarsus and began to wind its way northward up into the
Taurus Mountains. Following the perilous cliff road, it
passed through the famous Cilician Gates, a narrow cleft in
the mountains through which Alexander had once led his
victorious armies and through which the Apostle Paul and
his team had passed as they set out to evangelise Asia
Minor.

Beyond the mountains lay the high Anatolian plateau
and the air that night was already chilly compared to the
sticky heat of Adana. From a cloudless sky the moon
bathed the landscape in a ghostly brilliance, its light
reflecting on the shallow waters of a great salt lake as the
bus drew close to Ankara. The journey was only broken
briefly in a garage on the outskirts of the city, so Kenan had
to be satisfied with just a glimpse of Ataturk's great
mausoleum, picked out in the rays of the early morning sun
as they pulled away from the city.

It was one of those clear September Anatolian days in
which the sun shone from morning until night in a powdery
blue sky, and the rolling brown hills on either side of the
road stretched away to the horizon, the red roofs of
scattered villages standing out from the varied shades of
yellow and brown. Now and again village children in multi-
coloured skirts and baggy trousers would stop and wave as
the bus sped past.

Soon they were in the mountains again, the dusty plain
giving way to a carpet of evergreens and to high alpine
slopes kept green by rushing streams. From Bolu began the
long winding descent toward Izmit, where the flames from

the oil refinery pipes stood out even against the glare of the afternoon sun. During the last part of the journey between Izmit and Istanbul the road swept around the edge of the lake, and then by the Marmara Sea. The road was full of traffic, far more traffic than Kenan had ever seen in his life. Heavily-overloaded lorries ground their way up the inclines, sending out clouds of dense black smoke. Buses overtook each other on blind corners, seemingly oblivious to the hulks of wrecked vehicles by the side of the road, stark reminders that the *Mashallah* painted on the front of buses and lorries might not be all that was needed to ward off accidents. *Dolmushes* piled high with a day's shopping, and packed with sweating bodies, added to the general confusion, while the occasional private car picked its way cautiously through the mêlée.

For Kenan everything was different and exciting, but it was nothing to what his tired mind was faced with as the bus was carried on a ferry over the Bosphorous on the last stage of its journey to the European side of Istanbul, just thirty-six hours after leaving Midyat. In the evening sun a panoramic view of the city opened up before him as the ferry pulled away from the shore. On the Asian side of the city, fast falling astern of the ferry, the great Barracks of Scutari stood out from all the other buildings, its corridors once paced by Florence Nightingale when in use as a hospital during the Crimean War. To the right of the ferry the Bosphorous narrowed to no more than the width of a large river, curling its way up toward the Black Sea. To the left the sun was a great orange ball setting over the Marmara Sea, and ahead on the European shore a jumble of domes and minarets, towers and palaces, hotels and offices, rose up on either side of the Golden Horn. As they drew closer to the shore, the walls of Topkapi Palace – for centuries the home of the Sultans and their *harems* – loomed above them on their left. Below the palace on Seraglio Point at the mouth of the Golden Horn stood the very first statue of Ataturk to be erected – in its time a revolution in itself for a traditionally Islamic country in which all forms and images were previously anathema.

For the first time in his life Kenan set his foot on European soil. He thought that his journey had ended, but in reality it had only just begun.

The strange Assyrian

Early days at the Istanbul Boys' Lycée were overwhelming. At first Kenan did not like it at all. For a start there was strict discipline, totally different from the rather haphazard village atmosphere of Midyat. The standards at the school in Midyat had not been high – here he was stretched to the limit academically. In Midyat he had been a big fish in a little pond – somebody a bit special because of his family background; here he was a very small fish in a big pond and the transition was not an easy one. However, Kenan had a very friendly nature, a wide smile and an infectious laugh, and soon acquired a good circle of friends.

Apart from his rural roots, which were shared by others in the school, there were two other things about Kenan that singled him out as being different. One was his accent, which he could change with time; the other, his name, was more of a problem. In fact, it was only a matter of a few months before peer group pressure produced in him a passably respectable Istanbul Turkish accent. But what was this strange name 'Amanuel'? It was clearly not a Turkish Muslim name, so it was equally obvious that Kenan was not a Turk. What, then, was he doing in Turkey? Repeatedly Kenan was forced to explain his Christian origins, the background of the Assyrians, and the fact that they *were* part of the Turkish nation. It was both tiring and humiliating. Most Turkish boys brought up in rich, bourgeois homes in Istanbul were completely unaware that a people called the Assyrians existed. Their Turkey was the Turkey of the large westernised cities. Eastern Turkey was distant and unknown, its backwardness an embarrassment to a modern, progressive state. Since it was unacceptable, it had largely been ignored. So, from a schoolboy's perspective, these strange Assyrians came as if from another planet!

As if his name did not imply enough differences in race and culture, it was clear to all that Kenan could not be a true Turk because his religion was Christianity. As everyone knew, there were no Turkish Christians; such a concept was a contradiction in terms. During the Fast of Ramazan only two boys in the whole school went in for meals, Kenan and another boy from a Christian background. Many were the sneers and snide looks they received as they went off to enjoy their meals.

Furthermore, did Kenan not know, as everyone knew, that the *Injil* (New Testament) of the Christians had been changed at the Council of Iznik (Nicaea)? Every schoolboy was taught that there the Christian priests had been faced with the embarrassing discovery that up to several hundred conflicting *Injil* were in circulation. So, to solve the problem, they had all agreed on one edition, and burned the rest in a large bonfire. With such shaky beginnings, how could one compare the *Injil* to the glorious Qur'an, which had been sent directly to Mohammed from heaven by means of the angel Gabriel, and which had existed in Arabic, perfect and unchangeable, in heaven from all eternity? Furthermore, was it not clear that simple mathematical logic dictated that the God of the Christians was absurd since they apparently believed that one plus one plus one equalled one?

If there was one thing that Kenan hated, it was to be different from others. For the first time in his life he felt a deep alienation from those around him. Resentfully, he began to question why he had been born a Christian. He had not chosen to be. His family had never really read the Bible much or taken it seriously. He felt at heart no different from his Muslim friends. Their interests were his interests; their jokes were his jokes. He remembered the terrible tales sometimes told about the Turks by the older folk as they sat around the stove back home in Midyat during the long winter evenings. It was all absurd. After some of their city pretentiousness had been stripped off, these boys were just ordinary people like himself. Why should he be different? He felt in no mood to defend a religion he had not himself chosen and did not understand. What did religion matter, anyway?

After his first rather unhappy year at school Kenan discussed it all with his parents back in Midyat. There seemed only one solution – to change his name. So, by deed-poll dated 11 September, 1958, Amanuel took a Muslim Turkish name and became Kenan.

The effect back at school that year was dramatic. The major barrier to full acceptance had been removed. The release was enormous. To many of Kenan's Turkish friends, changing his name to one commonly used by Muslims was almost equivalent to becoming a Muslim. Indeed, Kenan began to read the Qur'an with some of his more serious-minded Islamic friends, and occasionally went with them to the mosque. At the same time his work improved and his teachers were very pleased with him that year. They wrote to his father: 'Your son is very quiet, his character is very clean, and he does not smoke like the other boys.' Enver was overjoyed. He approved of the school's emphasis on strict discipline and cleanliness. His proudest dreams for his eldest son were being fulfilled.

Sometimes the military atmosphere of the school became stifling. Officially boys were not allowed to go out and freely roam the streets of the city. The only permitted entertainment was a film shown inside the school every Saturday. Occasionally Kenan's uncle would come and take him out.

To vary the routine the older boys would often slip out unnoticed after classes were over and go down the road for a quiet smoke in the local tea-house, or spend a blissful few hours in the nearest cinema. At first Kenan was too timid to join in these escapades, but soon became as bold as the rest of them. Opposite the school were the offices of a major daily newspaper. One night Kenan and some friends were surreptitiously returning to school when a photographer from this paper slipped out of the building and took a picture of them in the act of climbing up a drain-pipe to the dormitory window. The next day their indiscretion was splashed over the front page as an example of the waywardness of youth, but fortunately the school authorities appreciated the funny side of the episode. Kenan had a great gift for disarming his critics in a friendly but forthright way, a gift that was to stand him in good stead during the years that lay ahead.

Though Kenan had in many ways rejected his Christian roots, there was a sense in which his Protestant heritage never rejected him. His language was a good bit cleaner than that of the rest of the boys, though he probably never stopped to question why. He found it difficult to cheat during tests with the same relaxed nonchalance affected by the other boys.

One night his friends persuaded him to go down to the well-known 'red light' area of the city. Kenan was well into his teens. It was, and still is, traditional in Turkish society for boys to visit brothels once they reach the age of sixteen to eighteen years. One of the unspoken duties of the eldest son in the family is to introduce the younger brothers to this practice at a suitable age. Although many may not go regularly, not to have gone at all is to cast a question-mark upon one's honour and manhood.

Kenan went along with the crowd, not wanting to hurt anyone in the group by saying 'no'. The street they came to was a dirty mean street full of small dingy houses. In each door was a small specially-hinged window, behind which the girls were waiting to display their 'wares' to newcomers. Kenan felt trapped. He wanted desperately to be part of the crowd, but deep down felt that something was very wrong. His friends split off in different directions and Kenan started towards the nearest door, but it was as if something strong inside had gripped hold of him. Memories stirred in his mind . . . something to do with God. He dimly remembered being taught that God was pure. He knew that what he was about to do was not pure, yet did not seem to have the power   himself to stop. But now he sensed that God had stopped him and turned him away. He did not know exactly why, but just knew that he could not do such a thing. He certainly had not thought much about God for months, but that day he became very aware that a higher power was somehow watching over him and protecting him.

Kenan hurried back to school.

The 1960 revolution

As the busy year passed inside the protective walls of the Istanbul Boys' Lycée, so the political forces that had been germinating since the 1950 elections (and before) were in their first stages of pulling the country apart. The walls of the school were not thick enough to keep out political ideas and philosophies, and the older boys began to discuss politics with the same passion formerly used to argue over their respective football teams.

The burning issues of the time were centred around the increasingly repressive policies of the Menderes government. Adnan Menderes, former lawyer and cotton planter, had swept to power with an overwhelming majority in Turkey's first truly democratic elections, held in 1950. At first everything had gone well. Turkish soldiers had fought with honour alongside the Americans in the Korean War, and Turkey had become a full member of NATO and the Council of Europe. But then the government had become increasingly repressive.

Part of the problem lay in the fact that a whole generation of leaders in the civil service, the universities, the judiciary and the media had grown up during the long rule of Ataturk and his 'heir', the Republican People's Party. The Democrats had been outsiders – businessmen, landowners and peasants – but now they were the ones in power. As the opposition became increasingly vocal, so the government reacted by stifling every form of criticism.

By 1957 army groups were conspiring to intervene in

politics and, though he did not know it then, the writing was clearly on the wall for Adnan Menderes. Politics had long been a passionate topic of daily conversation for the Turks, coming in a close second to sport as a subject that could arouse the most heat in the shortest possible time. But in the late 1950s, for the first time, masses of urbanised Turks began to become very involved in the political process. The heady wine of freedom which had been tasted through democratic elections was not now going to be lost to the heavy hand of authoritarianism.

Soon respectable Turkish parents, themselves reared in the disciplined society of Kemal Ataturk, were shocked to find their student offspring reading Marx and Lenin and engaging in political demonstrations. Some died in the ensuing clashes, though the number of people actually killed was tiny compared to the bloodbath that was to follow twenty years later.

Kenan was thoroughly involved in all that was going on and was beginning to feel very Turkish. He, too, began to read Marx. So much of it seemed to strike a chord; it was certainly true that a repressive regime was holding in check the wishes of the people. The only logical way forward seemed to be the way of revolution and the forceful overthrow of the government. It all seemed so much more practical than the mumbling of the priests back in Midyat. What had religion got to do with real life anyway?

In 1960 the Menderes government set up a special parliamentary commission to investigate the supposed sedition of the opposition. For the army and much of the general populace this was the last straw. The people took to the streets and for Kenan the sight of packed and excited crowds thronging the streets of Istanbul always remained a vivid memory. The image of a fellow school student being gunned down before his eyes in the clashes that followed was also to haunt him for years to come.

An army coup was now inevitable and the country was soon being ruled by a military junta. After a long and

protracted trial, Menderes and two of his Cabinet Ministers
were hanged. A commission was set up to write a new
constitution to ensure that future governments would
never again have such powers of repression. The final
constitution that emerged was full of guarantees for
freedom for almost anything, and for the very first time in
their history the Turks were promised, on paper at least,
true freedom of religious expression.

Article 19 stated: 'Every individual has freedom of
conscience, religious faith and opinions', whilst Article 20
continued: 'Every individual is free to express his thoughts
and opinions singly, or collectively, through word of
mouth, in writing, through pictures or through other
media'.

As the new constitution was unveiled with great fanfare
in 1962, Kenan read through the new clauses with the same
mild curiosity that most people had as they scanned their
newspapers that day. He had no idea then that those very
clauses would be so applicable and so relevant to his own
life just a few short years ahead.

5
New Life

Istanbul, 1962

Kenan's father wanted him to follow in his footsteps and train as a lawyer, but Kenan had other ideas. In 1962, he sat the Istanbul University entrance exams and achieved very high marks. These enabled him to go straight into the most coveted faculty of all – medicine. So in October of that year Kenan entered the Medical Faculty, but very soon found that earning high marks was no substitute for having an interest in the subject. Lost in a sea of physiology and biochemistry and repulsed at the thought of having to dissect dead bodies, he gave up medicine after only three months and applied instead to study civil engineering for the following academic year. Having high marks, there was no problem in making the transfer, and Kenan found himself with nine blissfully free months stretching before him.

Without all this free time, perhaps Kenan would never have found himself at a church just a few weeks after leaving the Medical Faculty. He had never been to church in Istanbul before, and in fact had no interest in doing so now, but a close friend of his called Shamun had arranged to meet a friend there and persuaded Kenan to come along. (Shamun was also from Midyat.)

The church they went to was called the Dutch Chapel, situated in a narrow street off *Istiklal Caddesi* (Independence Avenue), Istanbul's main commercial thoroughfare leading up to Taksim Square. After the service, Shamun found his friend whilst Kenan, in his outgoing way, was soon talking to two complete strangers who turned out to be foreigners – Roger and Dick. Unlike so many foreigners, they were very friendly and Kenan felt immediately drawn towards them. He offered to teach them Turkish, and in this simple way a friendship began that was to bring Kenan into a totally different way of life.

The first meeting took place in the home of Dick and his wife, Ruth. They were newly arrived in Turkey and their Turkish was very limited. Yet, as Kenan began to meet with them and other friends such as Roger, he soon noticed something about their relationships with each other that was very different from anything he had ever seen before; it was far more important for him than their occasional ignorance of certain Turkish customs. There was a kindness, a concern, and a genuine love that soon made a deep impression on Kenan. They not only cared for one another, they cared for him too as a person.

Kenan found something else about his new friends which was also very unusual. They believed in God, not as some distant outdated being who could readily be appeased by an occasional dose of religion, but as a closely personal loving heavenly Father with whom they talked as if he was standing right there in the room with them. Kenan could never forget the first time they prayed together and instead of the long heavy sonorous prayers that he connected with religion, out came short simple direct prayers, spoken in a normal conversational voice.

For the first time in his life Kenan began to read the *Injil* for himself. Knowing Arabic certainly helped in understanding the rather ancient Turkish used in the text. He started reading somewhat sceptically; after all, everyone knew that basically the message of the *Injil* and that of the Qur'an were the same . . . . While still at school Kenan had read enough of the Qur'an to know that it contained various laws and injunctions which he would never be able to keep. From all that he dimly remembered of stories in Sunday School, the Bible was rather the same – lots and lots of rules that were really not very relevant for university students growing up in a big city in post-revolutionary Turkey.

It took Kenan only a few days of reading to find that the message of the *Injil* and that of the Qur'an were poles apart. He studied seriously, carefully comparing what he knew of the Qur'an with parallel teachings in the *Injil*. One point was inescapable – the *Injil* was a book about love, the love of God in sending Jesus to die to take away sin; the love of Jesus as he hung upon the cross, praying for forgiveness for his tormentors; the love of the early disciples as they shared their lives together and turned the world upside down.

As Kenan steadily worked his way through the Gospels, he was startled to find that the person of Jesus was so totally different from the various stereotyped images he had in his mind from earlier days: the rather morbid figures of Jesus spread on the cross on the high altars of ancient Midyat churches; the anaemic pictures of a long-haired Jesus leading bands of sheep with sterile-white wool across the pages of ancient children's hymnals; the rather stern forbidding Jesus of vaguely remembered Protestant sermons at Easter and Christmas, sermons that told you all the things you could not do but nothing about new life. No, the real Jesus was nothing like that. And neither could he be the prophet described in the Qur'an, performing wonders it is true, but snatched up to heaven rather than being allowed the shame of the cross and the glory of the resurrection.

It was not long before Kenan realised that what he was reading was also being lived out before him in the lives of his new friends. They told him how for them, too, God had once been far away and inaccessible, but had become like a close friend once they had come to know Christ. They explained that there was no way you could approach a holy God on the basis of anything that you could achieve yourself. Having a respectable Protestant background did not help. All the penitent deeds of all the monasteries of the Midyat area put together were not sufficient to remove a single sin. All the prayers and fastings of all the mosques in Istanbul could not carry a sinner into the presence of a holy God. There was only one way, and that was the way God had chosen to break through into this world – by coming himself in the person of Jesus, who on the cross bore all the punishment for sin that was rightfully ours and who then, by bursting from the tomb, demonstrated once and for all that the power of sin and death had been destroyed forever.

God's true people were not those who adopted a certain religion, nor those who believed a certain creed, but those who, by personal faith in Jesus, had shared in his death and resurrection – death to the old life of sin, resurrection to the new life of power in the Holy Spirit – and who were right now living out a daily revolution of love as part of new communities of God's worldwide family, his Church.

What Kenan heard with his ears, so he saw with his eyes. These people had somehow experienced new power to say 'no' to something they knew to be wrong. They seemed to be free of that sickening sense of guilt and shame which came over him after he had lied or cheated, or like that dirty feeling that he had experienced after being in the red-light part of the city. This way seemed so different from the hypocrisy, the double-dealing and the pride in religion that he could see all around him, whether it was back in Midyat or right there in Istanbul.

After weeks of searching Kenan found himself face to face with the person of Jesus himself. Beside him all the teachings of Marx, all the revolutionary philosophies, all the secular materialism, all the mystical forms of Islam that had somehow seemed so attractive at one time, paled into insignificance. Kenan knew that he had to decide one way or the other about Jesus.

One day he read John 14:6 over and over again: 'Jesus answered, "I am the way and the truth and the life. No-one comes to the Father except through me." '

Could it be true? Could it be true that Mohammed was not the way, that the pious priests in the monasteries were not the way, that it was as simple as Jesus said? Kenan was suddenly overwhelmed with the realisation that either Jesus was telling the truth or he was a liar. But it was impossible that Jesus was lying – that certainly did not fit the facts. So Jesus *was* the way!

That day, quietly and with little emotion, Kenan prayed that Christ would take away his old life of self-centredness and give him a new life of love, the same kind of love he had already seen in the lives of his new friends. There were no flashes of lightning, no thunderbolts from heaven, but when he got up from his knees he knew that his life was never going to be the same again. The God of those early missionares to Mardin and Midyat, the God who had been worshipped by so many of his relatives as they sat waiting for execution in the prison that was now part of his home, the God of his grandmother who had prayed so long and so faithfully for him – this God had become his own heavenly Father, and Kenan had a strange feeling that he was coming home.

The spreading flame

How was it that foreigners like Dick and Roger had given up promising careers in their own countries thousands of miles away to come and live in Turkey?

During the late 1950s a prayer movement had begun in several universities and Bible colleges in North America. God had opened the eyes of several groups of students to the spiritual realities of a dying world. They had begun to meet for prayer, to spend long hours in intercession praying over maps of the world, especially those parts that remained largely unevangelised.

It was not only a prayer movement: it was also a protest movement. Many became sickened by the gap they saw between what the Church was preaching and what was actually happening in the lives of Christians. Every kind of sect and political group was struggling to reach the world with their particular ideology; yet Christians seemed content to enjoy their camp-fire choruses while the rest of the world burned. The radical teaching of Jesus in the Sermon on the Mount was comfortably designated to another dispensation; all the blessings of the gospel were preached Sunday after Sunday, but God's call for holy living and discipleship was quietly ignored.

Like every protest movement, it had its excesses, but the excesses were nothing compared to the spiritual sickness that gave rise to the protest. More and more students began to gather to pray, sometimes praying all night.

They soon realised that God did not want them just to sit on the sidelines – they had to get involved themselves. Soon groups of students were beginning to spend their summer and Christmas vacations in evangelism with local churches in Mexico. From there the vision spread to Spain and then the rest of Europe. Thousands of young people began to move out by faith to play their part in reaching the millions who were living so close, many of whom had never once heard the gospel, in the movement that eventually came to be known as Operation Mobilisation.

The main concerns in the prayer meetings through which the movement had been born, had always been the Muslim world and the Communist world. These two areas seemed to represent more than any other the great mass of the world's population that had received pitifully few opportunities to hear the gospel. Within a few years teams of young people began to move out of Europe to spend longer periods in these main target areas.

From the start Turkey had been a special concern for prayer. How could it be that the land so well evangelised by the Apostle Paul in the first century could be so neglected by the Church in the twentieth century? How could it be that there were only one or two known Turkish believers (as opposed to those of other backgrounds) in the whole country? How could it be that 35 million people (by the mid-1980s, 50 million) could live so close to 'Christian' Europe and yet be almost totally ignorant of the gospel? How could it be that in the dozens of places mentioned in the New Testament and now in modern-day Turkey (places like Galatia, Tarsus, Antioch, and the seven churches of Revelation), there was not a single known Turkish believer, let alone any churches? The situation seemed absurd. Something had to be done.

So Dick and Roger found themselves at the back of the Dutch Chapel on that rather cold wet Sunday in January 1963, where they first met Kenan. On their arrival in Turkey they had nothing like the backing, in numerical strength, of the great wave of missionaries who had come to the area in the previous century. But they did have other advantages. They were young, still in their early twenties, and so right on the wavelength of most Turks, since more than half the population was under the age of twenty-one. Furthermore, unlike their predecessors, they had the enormous advantage that they came with absolutely nothing that could be of material advantage to the people they were seeking to reach. They offered no aid; they were establishing no institutions; they were buying no property; they had no interest in enticing people away from their lifestyles and culture to an 'easier' life in the West. So it was far simpler to distinguish those Turks who had a genuine interest in the gospel from those who had listened with some ulterior motive.

As they settled in Turkey, it seemed unbelievable to Dick and Roger that they could find only one or two believers from a Muslim background in the whole country. Almost as incredible was the ignorance of real Christianity which they found as they talked to their new Turkish friends. Two whole generations had grown up almost totally unevangelised. The parents of the current younger generation had been raised in the secular climate of Ataturk's Turkey in the 1920s and 1930s, a time when evangelical witness had been largely extinguished by outright suppression on the one hand and by the inroads of liberal theology on the other. Despite the faithful witness of a few people and the steady though small outreach of the Bible Society, the new generation too had almost no opportunity to hear the gospel, especially the great bulk of the population that lived outside Istanbul.

The exceptions were those from nominal Christian backgrounds. As far as Istanbul was concerned these consisted of a dwindling population of Greeks, whose

numbers decreased as each new confrontation between
Turkey and Greece sent more scurrying across the Aegean
Sea; the Armenians, whose numbers were also decreasing
through emigration; and the Assyrians, whose numbers in
the city were in fact increasing at that time due to steady
migration from the Mardin area.

It was in this last group that Dick and Roger found the
greatest response to the gospel, especially amongst those
Assyrians who came from around Midyat. Kenan's great
friend, Shamun, also came to Christ and, within a few years,
a group of more than twelve had accepted Christ and had
started meeting together. Either as a direct or indirect
result of this witness, several hundred Assyrians have now
come into a living, personal faith.

Proving God

Despite his apparently phlegmatic exterior, Kenan was not
one to do things by halves. Having set his heart on
something, he was determined to see it through. From the
start his faith was patterned on the lives of his new friends
whom he admired immensely. If they read their Bibles and
prayed every day, well, so would he. If they took every
opportunity to share their faith, then that must be the
normal life for Christians, and it was the life for him too. If
they worked long hours for the sake of the kingdom, then
so would he.

The sceptic might think that a life so challenged by the
lives of others would fail once the initial challenge
disappeared. Not so with Kenan. Long after friends like
Dick and Roger departed from the scene, he kept on the
way he had started out.

The months that still remained before resuming studies
were now seen in a totally different light. Here was an
opportunity to invest his life where it would really count.
Taking a part-time job to support himself, Kenan began to
spend much of the remainder of each day helping his new
friends. It was a time when they were becoming very

involved in literature evangelism. Since there was almost
no evangelistic literature in Turkish, a start was made on
printing books and pamphlets. Kenan was appalled at the
prices that his new foreign friends were forced to pay by
different printers. Perhaps a Turk could obtain better
prices.

So knowing nothing about printers and printing, but with
an innate feel about how business should be done in his
native country, Kenan began to make his way alone around
the printers, gradually bargaining prices down.

The effects on the literature budget were dramatic.
Kenan began to obtain prices that were only half what the
rather naïve foreigners had been paying. So he soon found
himself running around Istanbul, involved in all kinds of
printing projects. Eventually, from these small beginnings
millions of Turks had the opportunity to 'hear' the gospel
through the printed page. In fact, not since the founding of
the Turkish Republic had such quantities of Christian
literature poured off Turkish presses, one of the fruits of
the new legal basis for religious freedom that had come
into being as a result of the 1961 constitution.

Everybody said that even to print such volumes of
Christian literature was quite impossible in a Muslim
country, let alone to distribute it. But, despite different
problems, the presses continued to roll, and a new and
rather ugly term became familiar to the readers of the
Turkish papers: '*Hiristiyan propagandaci*' (or 'Christian
propagandist'). Beneath banner headlines in the more
scurrilous sections of the press, pictures of the offending
printed items would often appear, complete with readable
text and follow-up address, which had the effect of
expanding the outreach considerably. The articles
invariably painted dramatic pictures of enormous foreign
organisations pouring money into Turkey aiming to flood
the country with 'Christian propaganda'. The readers of
these accounts would have been very surprised if they had
known that the great bulk of the Christian literature was
being produced on presses run by Muslim Turks, organised

by a young student from Eastern Turkey who himself had only just come to Christ.

For Kenan the joy of being practically involved in seeing the gospel go out was immense. No one told him that since he was such a young believer he would have to wait many years before sharing his faith effectively. From the outset it was assumed that he would be actively involved in evangelism, and so he *was*. As he became more involved, so his faith was stretched, and as his faith was stretched so he began to grow in Christ. This was part of the normal Christian life, not some special way reserved for the zealous few.

The move to Ankara

Kenan was so effective in helping the new literature work that after a few months as a Christian he moved to Ankara where his new friends had opened a Christian bookshop.

Until that time there had been only one Christian bookshop in all of Turkey and that was the Bible Society bookshop in Istanbul, which sold mainly Scriptures since there were hardly any other Christian books in Turkish to sell. To Dale, another of Kenan's close friends from his early days as a Christian, it seemed unbelievable that the whole nation should be served by only one Christian bookshop. Within a very short time another bookshop was opened in Istanbul, and then one in Ankara, the capital of Turkey.

Ankara was then, as now, the hard central core of Turkish resistance to the gospel. While Istanbul has always had a more cosmopolitan and European flavour to its daily life, if not to its scenery and architecture, Ankara since Ataturk, although having a more westernised and European exterior, is at heart solidly Turkish and nationalistic. There are the Parliament buildings, the ministries, the centre of the judiciary, the headquarters of the armed forces and, towering up in the centre of the city, the great mausoleum of Ataturk himself – symbolising a

Turkey freed from the intrigues of 'Christian' Europe, the invasion of the 'Christian' Greeks and the treacheries of the 'Christian' Armenians.

Although one-third of the population of Ankara were the more educated civil servants, teachers, students, businessmen and so on, holding to a politely humanistic form of Islam, the remaining two-thirds lived largely in the *gece kondu* (literally 'put up overnight'), the great area of cheap housing that had sprung up around Ankara as a result of a rather strange Turkish law legalising the building of a house provided its foundations were established within twenty-four hours. The inhabitants of these areas were flooding in from the villages in search of work and the great majority held to a more fervent and traditional form of Islam. But the fervent two-thirds and the more secularised one-third had something fundamental in common. They were Turks, and so they were Muslims. Every Turk was a Muslim and to be otherwise was unthinkable. In the whole city there were not more than a few hundred families at most from nominal Christian backgrounds.

The city of Ankara had remained almost totally unevangelised since the Christian community there had been largely wiped out in 1915. Before that, about two-thirds of the town's population had been nominally Christian. One lonely Bible Society colporteur had gone to live there in 1862 and remained faithfully distributing scripture portions for several years. As a result a small group of six believers had begun to meet at about the same time as a church sprang into life in Mardin. These believers continued to meet for fellowship in an incredibly harsh environment.

For some reason Ankara was renowned for its low moral state. A visitor called Mr Richardson wrote from there in 1867, speaking of the 'long day's ride from Gordium over wooded mountains' (mountains that are today sadly bare of trees) to an Ankara that was of 'unrivaled corruption and wickedness', and which 'scarcely had been more

debauched by drunkenness and wantonness in the days
when its temples of Bacchus and Cybele reeked of
revelling and lust . . . . Strong bodies of police patrol the
streets at night for the protection of families . . . .' In
contrast, the town at that time does not seem to have been
so daunting for the cheerful wife of the local British Vice-
Consul, whose writings tell of her house being 'furnished
with every English comfort', despite being 'so many days
from a railroad'.

However, her pleasing and sheltered life contrasted
sharply with the harsh realities often facing the local
population. In 1873-4 a famine devastated the area. There
were 18,000 deaths in the neighbourhood of the town
during the famine and 25,000 more people subsequently
died, together with sixty percent of the cattle of the area.
Children were found deserted and left in the streets and
some instances of babies being eaten by their parents were
brought to light.

Despite, or perhaps because of, the toughness of the
area, the evangelical church in Ankara had continued to
grow, and a man called Alexander was sent from
Constantinople to pastor the church. This fellowship had
continued until the massacres of 1915, when virtually all
the Christians of the town had either been deported to the
south or massacred. After that the church had never been
re-established.

It seems extraordinary that the Church in other lands
could draw so much benefit from Paul's epistle to the
Galatians, and yet show so little concern for Ankyra, the
ancient capital of the province of Galatia, which was now
Ankara, the modern capital of Turkey. Yet generations had
come and gone in the city without once hearing the gospel.

This was the city in which a small Christian bookshop
was opened in 1963, a critical test of the clauses
guaranteeing religious freedom in the new constitution.
This was the city to which Kenan came to join the handful
of foreign believers who had moved there, a tiny Christian
fellowship in a city known for its hostility to the gospel.

From the start the new bookshop received vehement opposition. It was one thing to open a Christian bookshop in Istanbul where, after all, there was a sizeable minority of Christians, but in Ankara . . . ? Since there were virtually no Christians in Ankara, this was seen as a sinister plot by the dreaded Christian propagandists to turn good Muslims from the true path and subvert the unity of the Turkish people.

Opposition to the new shop mainly took the form of police harrassment. For Kenan it was the first major test of his new faith. Standing as a Christian in cosmopolitan Istanbul was one thing, but here in this hostile city he felt alone and vulnerable. When the police saw Kenan in the bookshop, an intelligent young Turk, they became particularly angry. They shouted at him and threatened him, demanding to know why he was selling these lies.

In the same way that Kenan had hated to be different from his schoolfellows, he found it difficult to be disliked by others. He would do much to deflect anger and go the extra mile to pacify opposition. He knew that the books they were selling were perfectly legal. He knew that he was not breaking any laws by working in a Christian bookshop. Yet the jeers and threats continued. Sometimes the police took him off for questioning. Kenan wondered what his family would think if they found out. They had not been at all happy to hear that he had become 'religious'. Also he was afraid of how it might affect his future at the university. Perhaps the police would warn the university authorities about him and jeopardise his career? What if the police really let loose and gave him a good beating? Anything was possible.

At the root of these fears was a deeper, gnawing doubt. Was Jesus Christ *really* God? Was Jesus *really* more than just an ordinary man? If so, how was it that he, Kenan, was almost the only person in the whole city who believed this? Could it be possible that he had been deluded, and that the majority were right after all? And did Jesus *really* answer prayer? If so, why did these people continue to oppose

them, especially when they were meeting daily as a team to
pray.

Despite his doubts, Kenan continued working in the
bookshop, sharing with customers on every possible
occasion about the new life he had found. Finally, the
police became extremely angry about this 'young Turk'
who they thought had changed his religion. One morning
they came and arrested him. 'You didn't listen to our
warnings!' they said. 'Now we'll show you what we're going
to do to you. We'll get you thrown into prison. It'll ruin your
life; you won't be able to study anymore at the university!'
Kenan knew that these were no idle threats. A student who
spent a single night in prison for whatever reason could be
expelled from the university with no hope of re-entry.

The police handcuffed Kenan and led him away. There
was no hiding the fact that he was very scared. Suddenly he
saw all his life breaking up in front of his eyes. If he went to
prison he would not be allowed back into university. He
would not be able to be a civil engineer. His family would
be horrified. What was this new life he thought he had
found in Jesus Christ? How could God help him now? It
was impossible.

As Kenan was led out of the door, a friend of his, a
Dutchman, caught hold of him. He was someone Kenan
knew well; they had studied the Bible and prayed together
many times. 'Don't worry, Kenan,' he said. 'Just trust in the
Lord. He'll help you. I'll go home immediately and find
some others and we'll pray together for you.'

Kenan did not find this at all comforting. 'It's okay for
you to talk about trusting God,' he thought. 'You're not in
this situation. You're not Turkish. Your future isn't being
threatened. You're not handcuffed and being taken off to
court. It's hopeless!'

But the Dutch friend's words in fact touched him deep
down. Suddenly an image flashed into his mind of a
crowded prison in his own home back in Midyat. The year
was 1915 and the cellar was packed with believers joyfully
awaiting a fate that was surely worse than his. Why did

sacrifice seem so easy in past generations, but so very much more difficult in the present?

Out of these fears and conflicts came a weak, desperate prayer to God: 'Oh, God, if you really are God, if you really have become my heavenly Father, my Big Father, through Jesus Christ, please help me. Please rescue me from this situation. If you do, I promise that I will give you my whole life – I will live one hundred percent for you and do whatever you want.'

The police car screeched to a halt outside the *Adliye*, the Justice Building, a large grey ugly-looking edifice in Ulus, a commercial and business area of Ankara. Behind the building, steep cobbled streets led up to the Hittite Museum, and then to the walls of the ancient city perched on the hill above. Across the street, rows of cloth merchants and jewellers plied their trades.

The inside of the Justice Building was a hive of activity as various courts met in session and judges and lawyers bustled between the courts and the row upon row of offices that lined the long corridors. Louder even than the buzz of conversation was the chatter of dozens of ancient typewriters, each court having its own typist perched high up, just below the judge's panel, transcribing the proceedings at a furious rate. Set at intervals along the corridors were large bolted doors with sills curiously elevated several feet above the floor, which therefore had to be scaled by short ladders. These led not to prisons but to storage rooms, and through the occasional half-open door glimpses could be caught of stacks of forbidden literature, arsenals of all kinds of arms, and an accumulation of other confiscated items that clearly went back several decades.

Kenan was led handcuffed into the forbidding building, up two flights of stairs, along corridors, around a corner, right and up again. Finally, policemen and prisoner stopped before the door of the office of the judge who was to consider Kenan's case and decide whether he would be sent for trial. As they entered the room the policemen removed Kenan's handcuffs. The judge studied Kenan's papers with their long list of accusations.

'Name?'

'Kenan.'

'Surname?'

'Araz.'

'Birthplace?'

'Midyat, Mardin province.'

With this reply, the judge paused and looked up. After a second, he asked, 'Do you know Enver Araz?'

Kenan's heart missed a beat! He could not believe his ears. 'Yes,' he said. 'Enver Araz is my father!'

The judge's eyes lit up. 'I know your father very well. Some years ago I was sent by the government to work in Midyat. I worked alongside your father for three years. Many, many times I've been in your home.'

The judge started to look through the accusations. Then he turned to the secretary and the policemen guarding Kenan and asked them to leave the room. After they had closed the door he went over and embraced Kenan.

'Your family was so kind to me. It was just like my own home. They told me so much about you and how you were at school in Istanbul. What are you doing now? What's all this trouble about? Sit down. Tell me.'

So Kenan started to explain from the beginning how he had found his new life, how he had come to Ankara, the way in which the police had harrassed him and how he had prayed to God for help. The judge looked through the accusations again.

'These activities are not against the constitution anyway. We have no right to hold you.' In front of Kenan's astonished eyes, he tore the papers into shreds and threw the pieces into the waste-paper basket.

'Now,' he said, 'you must promise me one thing – you must come to my home for dinner tonight. And if you have any more trouble like this, you must contact me and I'll help you.'

How great is the love and power of God! Of the hundreds

of judges working in this huge building, Kenan had been led to the one who had worked in the insignificant town of Midyat more than 500 miles away. God had heard his feeble prayer and, minutes later, Kenan found himself walking out of the drab greyness of those musty corridors into the brilliant sunshine of an Anatolian spring day – free again!

Later the judge wrote to Enver Araz: 'It was very nice to meet your son, so grown up and with such a nice smile. We had such a nice chat.'

After receiving this letter and hearing of the whole incident, Kenan's father quite changed his views about his son's new 'religious friends'. Instead of spending his time warning Kenan against extremism, he became much more positive and later on when others from Midyat were imprisoned for their faith, it was Enver Araz who pacified the angry fathers who came to visit his home.

As for Kenan, it was a day he would never forget. God had proved his faithfulness. He *was* a loving heavenly Father who cared for the needs of very insignificant sheep. Jesus *must* be the way to the Father because he had answered prayer so directly and dramatically.

Kenan kept his promise. From that day on he pledged himself to live one hundred percent for God, fully, without reservation. And for the rest of his short life, that is exactly what he did.

6
Falling in Love

In October 1963, Kenan moved back to Istanbul to resume his studies, this time in the Civil Engineering Faculty. He decided to take the course in the evenings in order to leave time for evangelism and helping his friends during the day. Thus began a pattern of life that was to continue for the next few years, a life which was enjoyable but exhausting.

Early in the day Kenan generally went round to his new friends and they would have breakfast together, followed by a time of prayer and Bible study. During these informal fellowship times Kenan's knowledge of the Bible grew immensely and soon he was sharing his own insights from the passages they read together. But there was no danger of Bible knowledge becoming a substitute for action. For the rest of the day they would be out, often following up printing projects, or informally witnessing to people they met in the streets and parks, or else visiting different friends from the Midyat area who were also showing interest in the gospel. Several of these came to Christ and soon a small group was meeting regularly every week for fellowship.

Each evening Kenan attended his university course and, in contrast to medicine, took to civil engineering like a duck to water, often burning the midnight oil to complete his studies so that he could be free to help his friends the following day. At university he was accepted by most people as any other Turk, and Kenan soon had a wide circle of acquaintances. Some of these friendships with Muslims became very deep and led to opportunities for witness. Often he would go off with a whole group after lectures to some local tea-house, and not a few of Kenan's friends heard the gospel for the first time amidst the smoke-laden

hubbub of these places, drinking endless glasses of sweet
Turkish tea into the small hours of the morning.

Kenan liked being with a group very much, but one thing
he found very hard to bear was not having a girl-friend.
Living in Istanbul in a cloistered and well-disciplined
school was one thing, but mixing freely in the *laissez-faire*
atmosphere of the university was quite another. After the
tightly-controlled social structure of Midyat, where some
engaged couples still did not see each other until their
wedding day, Kenan found it hard to adjust to the free
atmosphere of the university. To add fuel to the fire, Turkey
was going through a social revolution in which contact
between the sexes was becoming much greater,
particularly in the big cities.

How nice it would be to have a girl-friend! Kenan knew
he could never marry a Muslim. This was not a conviction
that came firstly from his new faith, but something
engrained in him through his cultural upbringing. Everyone
knew that Muslims married Muslims and Christians
married Christians. To arrange things otherwise would
bring great shame and possibly danger to the families
involved. No, his girl would have to be a Christian – but
what kind of Christian? For the moment Kenan was not
particularly fussy. The main requirement was that she
came into his life as quickly as possible . . . .

Anda

About this time, in 1964, Kenan became very friendly with a
Greek family who were believers. The old father of the
family was still very active in mind and spirit. He used to
spend hours preparing a gospel calendar in Turkish with a
verse from the Bible for each day and a suitable comment
on the back of each page. He asked Kenan to help him with
this, so Kenan found himself going to the house more and
more often. With his own family so far away in Midyat, he
enjoyed the friendly family atmosphere of the home, and
particularly valued fellowship with the aging father who

had known and loved God for so many years.

It was during one of these visits that Kenan first learned of their beautiful young granddaughter, Anda. She was at that time in Cyprus, completing her secondary education. The father brought down her photograph from a shelf. Kenan's heart missed a beat! She was indeed a beautiful girl – a young fresh face, high cheekbones, a merry smile, hair swept back .... On future visits, between pages of the new calendar, his eyes would occasionally wander to the shelf where her photograph stood. Kenan liked girls with open, merry faces, not the ones that covered up and never even looked at you, like the girls in the more traditional families in Midyat.

At this time Kenan's Uncle Kerim and his family had just moved to Istanbul. Kenan had helped them to set up a small business and arranged for them to move into a small flat below this family with whom he had become so friendly. It was not long before the two families became good friends and their talk would often turn to the question of marriage for their various children and relatives. Then, as now, marriage was still largely a question of arrangement between parents, the children having more or less say depending on how traditional their family was. Certainly no children would think of marrying against the wishes of their parents.

Kenan was already twenty-four. It was time his family started negotiating for a bride for him. Although the practice of paying a bride-price was frowned upon by the government, the custom was still widely practised and even when not paid outright as a certain weight of gold, there were many substitutes for bride-prices that amounted to the same thing: agreements about furniture, living accommodation, and so on. Negotiations over such things could be long and tiresome, and would often be completed well in advance to ensure that a girl was 'booked' for the right man.

Yes, it was high time that Kenan's family started making a move. Discreet letters started to pass between Istanbul

and Midyat. Kenan also wrote to his father about the Greek
family. They were kind, he wrote, wealthy, and gave
excellent meals. Then there was the daughter . . . .

To both families it seemed an excellent match. Kenan
would graduate after a few years, with good job prospects.
Anda was nearing completion of her secondary education;
exactly the right time for a marriage to be arranged. By the
time she arrived back in Istanbul to rejoin her family, basic
agreement between the two families had already been
made. Kenan and Anda would be engaged as soon as they
got to know each other, and then marriage would follow
when Kenan was in a financial position to establish a
household.

When Anda finally returned in 1966, Kenan found that
the photo had not lied and so, with family backing and
approval, he had his girl-friend. She was seventeen.

Kenan, for all his zeal, boldness and growing knowledge
of the Bible, was still a young Christian. It had never really
occurred to him to pray much about his future life partner.
Disciplined in personal study, in relationships Kenan was
quite happy-go-lucky and took people much as they came.
With his natural and infectious optimism, he assumed that
everything would work out all right. No Christian books on
marriage were available to make him wonder whether they
were truly suited. He needed a girl-friend; she was both
friendly and good-looking, and the families favoured the
union. That was enough.

Not all Kenan's friends were so sanguine. Hristo was one
of them. Hristo had known Anda from the time she was
very small because he had stayed for some time with the
family. He also knew Kenan well. Every Monday Kenan and
some other believers would come to his house for a time of
prayer. Hristo had watched Kenan grow in Christ from his
early days as a believer. Deep down he was not happy with
the relationship, sensing that they were not really
compatible and fearing lest Kenan be deflected from
growing in the faith.

It was true that Kenan had vastly underestimated the

emotional and financial commitment of courting a rather demanding and good-looking teenager. He hated any meanness of spirit when it came to buying clothes, giving presents and entertaining, and soon found that he had to take a part-time job giving private tuition to supplement the money being sent from Midyat. Mr Araz himself was going through some difficult times financially. As the Assyrian population in the Midyat area continued to shrink due to emigration to Istanbul and Germany, so his clientele was growing ever smaller.

It was about this time that Kenan moved to share a flat in Osmanbey, an area of Istanbul not far from bustling Taksim Square. The flat was at the very top of a rather ramshackle building and life there was on the spartan side. Various members of the growing fellowship lived there at different times. One noteable character was a very tall and somewhat unshaven Assyrian who had made a profession of faith some time earlier and who insisted on praying in a very loud voice during his devotions, with occasional grunts and quivers to improve the overall performance, but who later fell away from the faith. The tall wooden triple bunk-bed that served as the sleeping quarters was infested with bedbugs, and the harmony of the diverse group was not helped by nights of scratching and beating off these marauders, which proved resistant to all forms of chemical warfare!

It was certainly nice, thought Kenan, to slip away to the pleasant surroundings of Anda's comfortable middle-class existence and, with the two families encouraging things along, the attractions of a free bachelor life gradually waned in comparison to the appeal of the more settled domestication of marriage. Besides, there was no doubt that status in Turkish society was radically different for a working man with a family as compared to a bachelor male student, a breed that in Turkey has always been viewed with some suspicion.

Engagement

In December 1966, Kenan and Anda were officially engaged
– engagement in Turkish society being viewed as only
slightly less binding than marriage itself. It was a very cold,
damp day, with a wet mist blowing in from the Marmara
Sea, yet a big crowd gathered to celebrate, including many
of Kenan's Turkish friends from the university. The rings
were exchanged, a singing group sang some of the new
hymns that had been translated into Turkish, and Anda's
uncle – a fine believer – gave a clear message about the real
meaning of marriage for two people who were committed
to God. The many Muslims present had never seen or heard
anything like it. For them it was puzzling to see how
religion could be brought so naturally into the heart of an
engagement party. In Islam, religion and party celebrations
were generally separated into comfortably watertight
compartments, certainly in the secularised form of Islam
prevalent in middle-class Istanbul society.

Kenan's parents could not be present at the engagement
because Midyat was so far away but his younger sister
Janet came up for the occasion. Already the change she had
seen in her brother's life had made a great impact upon her
and seeing her elder brother standing there so bold in his
witness before his Muslim friends made her feel very
proud. Later on she stayed for several months with a few of
the foreign Christian girls she met that evening who had
come to live in Istanbul, and for the first time in her life
began to pray and study the Bible herself.

After they had been engaged for a few months, Kenan
took Anda to Midyat to meet the rest of his family for the
first time. Not having had any advance warning of the visit,
his father was away. Kenan and Anda arrived in Midyat at
midnight when the heavy wooden door of the house was
well-bolted. They beat loudly on the door, but to no avail
since Mrs Araz had taken fright and hidden herself under
the bedclothes. Finally Janet heard the loud giggling from
the archway below and went down to let them in. So Anda

was introduced to the family and there followed a delightful few days of visiting relatives and riding in the surrounding countryside. A photograph remains: Kenan with broad beaming smile mounted on the family horse, with his arms around a smiling, slightly dishevelled Anda, also astride the long-suffering beast.

Life back in Istanbul was not quite so idyllic. The work load was by now extremely heavy. The university course took from four o'clock in the afternoon until ten. Frequently, after the lectures were over, Kenan would go and visit Anda in her home or take her out for a meal. After that there was often private study until the early hours and for a time Kenan found himself having to take pep pills just to keep awake. In addition there was by now a heavy programme of Christian meetings of various kinds. The situation was not helped by a diet that reflected the rather firm views on discipleship and simple living that were practised by his household, a diet in which rice played a prominent part.

Something else was wearing him down at this time, something that continued to be a trial and a burden for him until the very end of his life – the legalistic attitude of so many of the new believers in the Istanbul fellowship.

The growing church in Istanbul

As the Christian minorities continued to emigrate from Turkey during the 1950s and 1960s, so the membership of the few evangelical churches that remained dwindled. Most of these were in Istanbul. It was extremely difficult for them not to become introspective, feeling that they constituted a tiny island of Christianity in the midst of a threatening Muslim sea. The main task, they felt, was to strengthen the ramparts, keep the faith, and make sure that their children were brought up with some knowledge of the Bible. The idea of a local church of Turkish people from a Muslim background was simply unthinkable. Though at various times Turkish believers had gathered for meetings in different parts of the country, notably in the mid-nineteenth century, there had never been a truly local Turkish church. The great majority of Armenian, Assyrian and Greek believers equated the continuation of their churches closely with the fortunes of their communities. No one seriously believed that Turks could be converted anyway . . . .

So the ninety-nine percent Muslim majority in the country, largely Turks with a big minority of several million Kurds and many smaller ethnic groups as well, remained totally unevangelised. In contrast to previous centuries, when at least Christians from the minority groups had risen to prominent positions in society, the new Republic was monolithically Turkish and therefore Islamic. There was no Christian member of Parliament to put in a kind word on behalf of Christians. There were no Christians in the legal profession, the universities or the arts. There were no Christian journalists, authors, or doctors. In short, there was no salt. It was as if Paul had never gone there; as if his letters to the Christians of Galatia, Ephesus and Colosse, and the messages to the other churches of Asia Minor as related in Revelation, had never been written. Nothing remained but dead stones.

Those whom God had told to preach the gospel in Turkey could not accept this. For them the gospel was not something that could be bottled up in a particular cultural community. God loved Turks as much as he loved Armenians or Greeks. He was not biased towards a nation just because it was the first ethnic group (like the Armenians) to turn as a nation to Christianity. Jesus died for *all* men and all equally could come to saving faith in him.

So those Christians from different countries who went to take the gospel to Turkey in the early 1960s spent as much time witnessing to Muslim Turks as they did to those of other backgrounds. But it was mainly those like Kenan, from an Assyrian background, who actually came to Christ at the beginning. There were some Turks as well, but many

of these had various kinds of struggles and relatively few
continued in the faith.

As more and more Assyrians came to Christ, not
unnaturally the regular meetings began to take on
something of an Assyrian flavour. Though the worship was
in Turkish, it was not uncommon to hear Syriac, Greek or
Armenian spoken during the fellowship that followed. It
was, indeed, a 'people movement', consisting largely of
Assyrians from a small network of villages in the Mardin
area whose families had migrated to Istanbul. Friends
introduced the gospel to those who had come from the
same village. Mutual acceptance was made easy for most
because they came from very similar backgrounds.

While this people movement had the advantage that it
penetrated quite rapidly into the Assyrian community in
Istanbul, it had the disadvantage that this community was a
tiny minority among the vast majority of Turks. This meant
that on those occasions when a Turk came to the meeting,
it was like stepping from his own culture into something
strange and non-Turkish. There were barriers enough as it
was between Islam and Christianity without the added
alienation of having to adapt to the ways of a minority
culture. For this reason some Turks who expressed
interest in following Christ and came to one or two
meetings soon stopped coming.

The new monasticism

After his years in Istanbul, Kenan felt Turkish enough to
know how off-putting some of the meetings could be for
newcomers. But there was something far deeper which,
from the beginning, seemed to run through the life of the
growing church and which was, for Kenan, very disturbing.
It arose directly from the fact that most of those being
converted were from Orthodox backgrounds and this
continued to influence strongly their concept of what the
Christian faith was all about.

Anybody who had visited one of the lengthy services in

the monastery near Midyat and who had then visited one of the meetings of the growing church in Istanbul, would readily be able to detect certain similarities. Though the words of the new church were Protestant, the concept of the monastic ideal still ran deeply through the life of the fellowship. For example, it was not enough to pray in a normal voice – praying was best carried out in a special 'holy' voice, preferably full of verbose and flowery spiritual phraseology. Christianity was a solemn affair and therefore any levity in meetings was rapidly squashed. Being spiritual was equated (as in certain churches in other countries) with a very long list of 'don'ts', and the salvation of anyone who smoked, drank or went to the cinema was definitely suspect in the eyes of most. Since Christians were only pilgrims on the earth, clothing was deemed to be of secondary importance and those who considered themselves spiritual would therefore cultivate a somewhat seedy appearance. Illnesses were seen in general to be due to sin and therefore repentance was considered to be the correct response for the sick Christian, who should call upon the church to pray for him rather than upon the services of a doctor.

For Kenan all of this was anathema. He had a simple but direct faith, and although his upbringing had lacked a firm biblical foundation, it was Protestant enough to give him a deep suspicion of complicated religiosity. God was a big, loving, heavenly Father, who longed for every prodigal son to return to him. Salvation was by repentance and faith and was through the finished work of Christ on the cross – plus ... absolutely nothing. The grace of God was available not just to enter the kingdom, but to live every day as a Christian. No amount of religious observances could add one jot or tittle to one's status as a child of God. Worship was not the obligation of a religious performer but the spontaneous joy and praise of a saved sinner. Jesus came to give life, abundant life – not to turn life into a new but drab set of rules and regulations. Christians were people who were pro-life, not those who abhorred this present life as if human existence itself was somehow only peripherally part of God's redemption.

These two contrasting views of the Christian faith both had very long pedigrees and it was inevitable that they should clash in the lives of Kenan and those whose views differed from his, just as they had clashed in Galatia in the first century and in so many other of the early churches.

For Kenan, the problem was compounded and confused by the question of class and up-bringing. Though he came from the same area as many of the others in the growing church, there was no hiding the fact that he was from a well-known, upper middle class Protestant family which at least in earlier years had been comfortably well-off, in sharp contrast to the poor farming Orthodox families from which most of the other new believers came. Furthermore he had spent long years of education in one of Turkey's best schools and, to cap it all, now had a Muslim name which, in the eyes of some, already made him suspect.

Kenan's relationship with Anda brought everything to a head. Anda was pretty, vivacious and, as far as many in the fellowship were concerned, worldly. Worst of all, she wore make-up and she and Kenan had even been seen going out together before they were yet married! Gossip is a great destroyer and it was not long before gossip began to break down Kenan's fellowship with some of the others. He was labelled *hafif*, Turkish for 'light', someone who did not have a serious enough view of the faith. 'Kenan is a good brother,' they would say, 'but you know he . . .', and then would come the juicy descriptions to further prove that he had reached the dreaded state of being *hafif*.

Once Kenan and Anda went to a party at which there was some dancing and this led to a big wave of gossip, culminating in a meeting of most of the fellowship at which some called for Kenan's expulsion from the church for his great 'crime' of association with the 'world'.

Kenan maintained an extraordinary lack of bitterness throughout these events. It would have been so easy to have reacted and to have written off these accusers as a collection of hypocrites, but this Kenan refused to do. Though often hurt, he somehow maintained his sweetness of temperament, a big loving heart in which there was no room for any 'root of bitterness' to grow. God was a lovingly heavenly Father who welcomed into his family all who were joined to Christ. So, 'Welcome one another as Christ has welcomed you,' he would remind his accusers. 'There is so much that unites us. Let's talk about those things, not the secondary issues that only bring division.'

It was Kenan's simple but deep conviction that God is love, and that any fellowship not reflecting something of that love is out of tune with the character of God. More than that, his heavenly Father loved him, Kenan, personally and to such an extent that he had called Kenan to himself out of millions of others. The least that he could do was to walk daily in that love.

Whether he would continue to walk in that love even when his fiancée, his health and his education were all stripped from him was a question that still remained to be answered.

7
Slide towards Death

Kenan's breakdown in health was insidious and at the
beginning went largely unnoticed. Some close friends, such
as Hristo, remarked that he had looked very pale the first
time they had met him in the early 1960s, but put it down to
overwork. When Kenan used to go home to Midyat for
holidays, his family would complain that city life was doing
him no good. They tried to feed him up with great plates of
kôfte (meatballs), *bulgur* (cracked wheat) and yoghurt, but
still Kenan's complexion maintained an ominously yellow
tinge.

One doctor in Istanbul was convinced that the problem
was worms, and prescribed large brown bottles of
powerful anti-worm pills. Despite two courses of this
obnoxious medication – which certainly had some very
direct effects upon the digestive system and which would
have undoubtedly finished off even the toughest of Turkish
worms, had they been present – Kenan's health remained
much the same.

The pressure of the daily programme was just as great.
Large teams were involved in distributing literature in
different parts of the country. Millions of Turks were
hearing at least something of the gospel for the very first
time. Thousands began to enroll in a Bible correspondence
course. All these forms of outreach meant more printing
projects and Kenan was by now becoming an expert in
organising literature production.

Opportunities for sharing the gospel abounded, but
sometimes at the end of the day Kenan found that he hardly
had the strength to drag himself up the endless flights of
steps to the top-floor flat in Osmanbey. Even the thought of
taking out Anda palled when he felt so tired.

One night after taking Anda home, Kenan became very ill. Anda's family called a doctor, but no clear diagnosis was made. Kenan was packed off to Haseki Hospital for a thorough check-up. The tests carried out there proved conclusively that the root cause of his deteriorating condition lay with his kidneys. To Kenan's surprise he found himself entering the hospital on 17 October, 1967 for what turned out to be a stay of nearly three months.

God's Bible school

With a sudden jolt the relentless programme of Kenan's hectic life came to an abrupt halt. He was suffering, apparently, from nephritis. The term itself was strange and at the beginning he had only the vaguest idea of how serious it might be. What he did know was that the special diet the doctors soon placed him on was low in protein, saltless and tasteless. Kenan's stomach was always very close to his heart and the new diet excluded all his favourite dishes.

'How can I eat this awful stuff!' he complained many times. Then one day he saw a picture of starving people in India and was shocked at how easily he had allowed himself to slide into selfishness. Those people had nothing. At least, thought Kenan, he had some food to eat, however unpalatable. Gradually he began to learn how to give thanks again.

So came about the first small victory in a battle that was to continue for many years – the struggle to prevent a root of bitterness growing up in the fertile ground of apparently meaningless suffering. What happened to Kenan in Haseki Hospital was like the skirmishes of a larger war that was yet to come and the small victories won there led to bigger victories later on.

It was a time for reflection, a compulsory pause in a life that had become too full. During the quieter moments Kenan would stare out over the rooftops as the long warm autumn days of October and November gradually gave way

to the clammy dampness of December, and boisterous
winds frisked the leaves off the trees almost before they
had time to change colour. Then came the snows, not the
powdery fresh snow of the Anatolian plateau, but wet
slushy snow driven hard by northern winds that turned the
streets to mud and set the dolmushes sliding and skidding
up and down Istanbul's steep cobbled streets.

Anda – what about Anda? Many times Kenan's thoughts
would turn to her as he lay in hospital. Often she would
visit, immaculately dressed, cheerful, her passage down
the row of beds followed by inquisitive and admiring eyes.
But as she looked at Kenan lying there, a shadow seemed to
pass over their relationship. How long was the illness going
to last? Was marriage a realistic option for someone
confined to a hospital bed for so long?

For Kenan, ever the optimist, these questions were of
relatively minor importance. He was quite sure he was
going to get better. True, he was missing several months of
university, but some heavy cramming would make it up. He
had deeper doubts, however, about his relationship with
Anda. Too many close friends had told him that they were
not suited for each other, that their marriage was not God's
will. But how then could he feel so good whenever she was
around? During the long boring evenings Kenan turned
these thoughts over and over in his mind, but there seemed
no easy answer.

Christian friends of various nationalities came to visit
frequently. The nurses used to joke that Kenan's ward was
becoming like the United Nations. His flat-mates were
faithful visitors. Other old friends such as Dale and Roger
could no longer come because the Turkish Government
had forced them to leave the country.

These deportations were a curious phenomenon on
which Kenan would often ponder. The Turkish
constitution had guaranteed religious freedom since 1961.
According to both the laws of the country and the
constitution it was perfectly legal to share one's faith
verbally or through books and films. The distribution of

Christian literature was completely legal. Furthermore, these rights were the same for both Turks and foreigners for, according to the constitution, all were equal before the law.

So why did the Turkish Government insist on deporting foreigners who shared their faith? Typically, a neatly-typed police order would arrive informing the person that his residence permit had been revoked and that he should leave the country within twenty-four hours, with no reasons given. There was no hope of that person ever living as a resident in Turkey again. A note had been made in their file in the Ministry of the Interior in Ankara and any further application for residence permits would be turned down.

Of course every country had the right to deport foreigners who broke the law – Kenan did not need to be the son of a lawyer to know that. But the yawning gap between paper principles and daily reality seemed excessive in this case. If Turkey wanted to be a purely Muslim country, after the fashion of most other countries of the Middle East, with no guaranteed religious freedom to share one's faith, etc., then why not state it clearly? But if Turkey wanted to be a truly European country – which is what Ataturk's revolution was all about – then why not actually practise the claims to religious freedom that were embodied in the constitution?

Although for Kenan the legal contradictions of deportation were puzzling, it was the loss of close friends that distressed him most. However, others came to take their place. Steve and Diane and their family soon won a special place in Kenan's heart. A one-time snack-bar worker who had drifted into taking hard drugs as a teenager before his conversion did not seem on paper the best candidate to go and help evangelise Turkey – but such was Steve's background. Lacking the latest missiological degrees, Steve nevertheless had the far more important qualification essential to anyone working in Muslim countries – a warm, outgoing friendly spirit that quickly won people's affection and confidence. Kenan, who also had an innate suspicion of anything overly complex and theological, warmed immediately to the simple faith of Steve and Diane, and their children soon loved him as a cheerful and indulgent uncle. When they came to visit him in hospital they were like a bright and encouraging light in a dismal room.

The visits of some of the national believers had the same effect. They would laugh, chat and pray together, and Kenan's spirits would be uplifted. But the visits of another group of believers were quite different. At times they were rather like Job's comforters.

'Brother, we are truly concerned for you as you lie here in the hospital when you could be out actively serving the Lord.'

'Of course.'

'We're missing you in the fellowship – it's sad that you can't meet as usual with the Lord's people.'

'I would love to be there.'

'And of course the Bible says that those with real faith should simply trust God for their health and not put themselves in the hands of these butchers [doctors]. Search your heart, brother; it's clear there must be some hidden sin or fault, and that God has brought this upon you to show you the error of your ways. Repent and then the sickness will leave you.'

So the sermonising would continue, on and on, while Kenan listened politely, his mind in such a whirl afterwards that he could hardly sleep. Perhaps they were right? Perhaps he had not yet attained the right spiritual plane so that he would be released from this bondage of illness? During these times of doubt the heavy religiosity of the Mardin monasteries, steeped in neo-platonic views about the evils of the body compared with the value of the soul, would sweep over him like a dark black cloud.

One morning Kenan was happily telling the patients around him about the new life that he had found in Jesus. Suddenly one of them piped up: 'Well, if your God is so great, why are you ill in hospital?' Kenan stopped short. For the moment he had nothing to say. Here was the same fundamental objection, only presented in a slightly different way. What the Job's comforters were saying was clothed in respectable evangelical language, but the direct, blunt question of this Muslim was making the same basic point. The first were saying, in effect, that God did not really love him and was punishing him for something he had done wrong. The Muslim was saying that God could not love him anyway, since if he really did he would not allow Kenan to apparently waste his life lying in a hospital bed.

Kenan did the sensible thing. With time on his hands, he searched the Scriptures. Gradually light dawned. James 1:2-4 was a particular help. His illness was not sent by God. Nothing evil could come from God anyway. God did love him, but he was willing to allow trials to come into his life to test his faith and develop Christian perseverance and character. The end result was to be 'mature and complete' in Christ.

Hebrews 12:1-12 was also a great encouragement at this time. Sonship for Kenan was not a bed of roses anymore than it had been for the Son of God himself. But the whole point of trials and of discipline was that they might lead to 'sharing in God's holiness'.

As Kenan began to understand the Scriptures more, so he began to rest in the assurance of God's love. Ever since his dramatic release in Ankara, he had known that God had a personal concern and interest in every detail of his life. Now that conviction was clothed with a greater biblical understanding. He found that he could witness with more confidence, because he could not only state the fact of God's love, but also the scriptural reasons underlying that fact, while being able to relate it to what he was experiencing himself.

At the same time it did not take Kenan much more reading of the Bible to see that God never in fact promised that believers would not be sick, and even less that calamities and sickness were forms of punishment for sin.

The teaching of Jesus was perfectly plain on the second point, as he made clear in his replies concerning the man who was born blind (John 9:1-7) and the people crushed by the falling tower at Siloam (Luke 13:1-5).

As for the question of healing, Kenan had not the slightest doubt that God could heal people in the absence of modern medicine if he so wished, but he could find no biblical basis for the idea that one should spurn doctors and medicines. Medicines were just as much a part of God's creation as food and clothing and were to be received 'with thanksgiving' (1 Tim. 4:4).

And what hint was there that *all* the blessings of the 'age to come' were the birthright of every believer right now? The New Testament indeed gave the picture of the kingdom of God breaking right into the 'present evil age', with demons being cast out and sicknesses being healed (Luke 11:14-20), but the whole point was that Christians were called to belong to two ages *both at the same time*. Temporally they were still part of the 'present evil age', though they had been rescued from the power of its grip (Gal. 1:3,4), but in spiritual allegiance and by the indwelling of the Holy Spirit they actually belonged to the 'age to come' (Eph. 1:19-23).

The clash between the two ages was like two strong ocean currents flowing into each other, with the water in turmoil at the point of collision. Believers were called to live at the point of tension, in the centre of the turmoil. There was no doubt which current was ultimately the stronger, but until Jesus came again to complete his destruction of the kingdom of darkness, the conflict would continue. All the future blessings of the kingdom were no more the present possession of believers living on earth than were their resurrection bodies, a point apparently missed by Hymenaeus and Philetus (2 Tim. 2:17,18).

This was why apostles such as Paul fell ill like other mortals, even evil things like disease being used in the sovereignty of God to see new churches established in first century Turkey (Gal. 4:13,14). This was why Paul's fellow-workers, such as Epaphroditus and Trophimus, were not always automatically healed (Phil. 2:27; 2 Tim. 4:20). This was why chains and suffering were always part and parcel of a faithfully-witnessing church (Phil. 1:14,28,29). This was why servants of God sometimes had their houses taken from them (Heb. 10:34), or suffered from hunger, sleepless nights, beatings and imprisonments (2 Cor. 6:4-6). This was why believers were sometimes killed (Acts 12:2).

It was quite a different Kenan who was finally discharged from Haseki Hospital on 6 January, 1968. He felt as if he had been to Bible school – God had taught him so much during those three months. Now there was not so much time for Bible study, but the Scriptures stayed in his heart and mind and a permanent spiritual impact remained from his time there.

Live like a vegetable?

Though Kenan emerged from hospital rejoicing in spirit, his body felt weaker than when he had entered, the effects of the enforced rest having been offset by the results of eating such a low-protein diet. Every day he had injections, but they seemed to do him little good.

A few weeks later an opportunity suddenly opened to visit a specialist in Germany. He confirmed that Kenan was suffering from chronic nephritis. Was a kidney transplant a possiblity? Perhaps because at that time transplants were relatively rare and the long-term effects had been little studied, the doctor replied that if Kenan did have a kidney transplant he would not be able to work, but would 'exist like a vegetable'. Another possibility would be to live on a kidney machine, but this was very expensive and probably not available in Turkey. The only solution was to keep to a special diet.

Surprisingly Kenan came back from Germany remarkably cheerful. Deep down, he had the hope that things were going to work out differently, that the doctor's gloomy predictions were going to be refuted, and that his

'Big Father', as he delighted to call God, was going to look after him and eventually restore his health.

An inner conviction was already beginning to form – a kidney transplant was the only way. Logically everything was against it: he had no money; transplants were not being carried out in Turkish hospitals at that time; and the possible outcome of a transplant sounded ominous anyway. But his 'Big Father' was going to work it out – of that Kenan had no doubt.

There were two immediate results of Kenan's trip to Germany. One was that Anda's family began to question him closely about his health. There was no hiding the gravity of the situation and the family was shocked as they began to understand the facts. How could their daughter marry someone who was likely to die so soon? How could a person as ill as Kenan be the head of a household? The objections came thick and fast. Logically they were sound, but both Kenan and Anda began by fighting the inevitable decision. They would manage somehow. They still loved each other. The doctor might be wrong anyway . . . .

But after some further pressure, the decision was accepted. The engagement was broken off and the deeper doubts that Kenan had felt about their relationship before were suddenly resolved for him in a way that he had never expected. Yet it was a bitter blow. Dying from kidney failure was something in the future, something that might not happen anyway. The sudden break with Anda had to be suffered immediately and an aching void was left in his life.

As for his own family, they did not learn until much later the serious nature of the illness. Conforming faithfully to Turkish custom at this point, Kenan deliberately kept the German doctor's verdict from them, always planning to tell them once he had completed his studies two years later.

The second immediate result of Kenan's trip to Germany was that he went to live with Steve and Diane. The doctor had given him a thick dietary book full of complicated instructions in German, and it had soon become clear that this would have proved too taxing for a bachelor

household. What Kenan needed was plenty of motherly
love and someone who was firm enough to keep him to his
diet: this was precisely what Steve and Diane proceeded to
do. Not only that, but they decided to move house so that
Kenan could be nearer to the university.

Finding a flat to rent in Istanbul was a tedious and
lengthy operation, especially if you were set on living in a
certain area of the city. Every day Steve would scour the
streets near the university, craning his neck to look up for
the tell-tale signs of empty flats – the absence of curtains
Kenan was also looking as he walked to lectures each day.
One evening they both came back, each having found the
ideal flat, only to find that it was the same one! But first the
landlord and, even more importantly, his wife, had to 'look
them over' to make sure that they would be suitable
tenants.

The following evening Steve and Diane went over for a
visit. The evening was going well and prospects of renting
were looking very hopeful when Steve said: 'By the way, it
will be our family, our two children, and a young Turkish
man who will live with us.'

There was a sudden silence. The landlord's expression
changed. A single Turkish man? That was different. The
presence of a single man would not enhance the reputation
of the building. Besides (though he did not say this) the
landlord had a young eligible daughter and since the rented
flat was just below theirs, they had to think of her safety
too . . . . The silence was broken as the landlord said: 'Well,
in that case, I'm very sorry, but it won't be possible after
all . . . .'

Without even looking at each other, both Steve and
Diane had a sudden inner conviction that God wanted them
to have this flat. Though Steve's Turkish was still not the
best, he quietly began to explain how Kenan was different:
'But you don't know this man. He's not just a Turk – he's my
brother. He's ill, and may soon die if we don't look after him
properly. We *must* have Kenan with us!'

As Steve said this both he and Diane spontaneously

started to cry. The Muslim landlord and his family were deeply touched. They had never before seen foreigners like this who obviously cared deeply for the welfare of an insignificant young Turkish student. The very presence of God seemed to permeate the room. Tears touched them at a level that arguments could never reach. After a little more discussion, the decision was made: Kenan could come too.

So, a few days later, Steve and Diane moved with their enlarged family into the flat that God had so clearly provided. In the event, Kenan quickly won the hearts of the landlord and his family, and later on had many opportunities to share the gospel with them.

Slide towards death

Kenan soon settled into the new pattern of life. He immensely enjoyed the loving comfort of being with a family, but the next two years proved the hardest yet.

For a start there was no Anda. Kenan would often talk with Steve when he came home in the evenings of his near desperation to get married. There were so many nice Turkish girls at the university, but he knew that he could never marry any of them; not just because he was so sick, but because they did not share the same faith. Kenan had learned a lot in this area since his engagement with Anda. He knew now that the Bible was perfectly clear that a Christian should only marry another who had the same personal faith in Christ. But it seemed that as the theory became clearer and clearer, so the practice became harder and harder.

For a time Kenan became deeply depressed. His life consisted almost entirely of going to lectures and then conserving every bit of remaining energy to complete his studies at home. As 1968 slipped into 1969 he could feel himself progressively growing thinner and weaker. Diane was wonderful at helping him keep to his diet and this did much to keep the headaches at bay, but the lack of protein was continuing to exert its toll.

In fact very few people understood then how very ill he was, partly because Kenan talked little of what the German doctor had told him. Sometimes he became frightened at his condition. His face seemed to grow paler and thinner each day. Later he joked about this time: 'My face was so yellow, I searched everywhere in Istanbul to find a mirror that would make me look normal!' But deep down Kenan knew he was dying.

Sometimes the Job's comforters came by, still pressing home the same old message. In fact 'going to pray with Kenan' became quite a feature of life for some of the local fellowship, particularly when he was too ill to attend meetings. But what this actually meant was not a visit to encourage a sick brother, but a kind of accusatory session during which other believers tried to find some sin in his life that was causing his condition. They were praying for his healing, but it was always linked to the conviction that Kenan was hiding 'secret thoughts' preventing God from working. So the cloud of condemnation would grow and grow.

Kenan was even told that it was God's judgment upon him that Anda was not now going to marry him. This last accusing arrow came particularly from those who had shown signs of jealousy at his engagement to such an attractive girl.

It is remarkable that still Kenan did not allow these barbs to make him bitter. Steve and Diane said that he had a character like that of Nathanael – he was 'without guile'. Rather than growing angry at the constant stream of accusations, he would take them seriously, search his own heart, and often kneel with the visitors to pray with them that God would keep his heart pure and search him for any 'secret faults'.

Often the reproving fingers would drive Kenan towards despair. But he always came back to the bedrock of the promises of Scripture. The lessons learned in Haseki Hospital had not been forgotten. God loved and accepted him just as he was – a weak, failing, repenting sinner. That was the basis upon which Christ accepted him and that was the only basis upon which Christians should accept one another (Rom. 15:7). In his heart he might feel 'the sentence of death', but this would help him to rely more on 'the God who raises the dead' (2 Cor. 1:9).

Together with the promises of Scripture there was one great hope that helped to pull Kenan out of his depression – the possibility of a kidney transplant operation. The conviction grew in his heart that one day he would indeed have a transplant and that his new kidney would come from his mother, but at that time he told no one of this inner intuition.

A few close friends began to investigate the possibilities of kidney transplants abroad. The information that began to come back was not encouraging. Germany would be wildly expensive. If it was going to be anywhere, England seemed to be the best place, though there also enormous sums of money would be required, and there was a long waiting list.

It all seemed quite impossible. In early 1969 Diane was expecting her and Steve's third child. Kenan felt he was being too much of a burden upon them, so in the spring he moved out and found himself living once again in a bachelor flat. As a place to live, it had little to commend it. Situated on the fourth floor, up many flights of stairs, it had the added disadvantage that it was without water most of the time since the water pressure was rarely sufficient to reach the upper floors. So all water had to be carried up by hand. The kitchen was a small pokey place infested with cockroaches.

It was hardly an encouraging place to live for someone with terminal kidney failure.

By the summer of 1970 Kenan had just a few months of studies left before graduation. Final exams were looming on the horizon. After all those years of hard work, the long course in civil engineering was almost complete, the course that had been made even longer by his enforced stay in hospital. He decided to have a break in Midyat before the final slog leading up to the exams.

Kenan's family was shocked when they saw his changed appearance. They pressed him for details of the illness, but Kenan was loathe to come out directly with what was wrong. However, he confided a little more fully with his sister Janet, and she made a wild suggestion: 'Take me with you to Istanbul! If my kidney is suitable, I'll give it to you immediately! If you don't want to make the family worry, just take me and later, if it works out, you can explain to the family . . .'

Kenan hardly relished the thought of sending his sister back home minus a kidney without having obtained the family's permission, and fortunately common sense prevailed.

Finally he told his parents everything the German doctor had said and that a transplant seemed to be the only hope. Far from the news crushing them as Kenan had feared, they seemed quite optimistic when they heard of the possibility of a transplant. Total ignorance of the complexities, dangers and expense of having such an operation prevented them from seeing what a far-fetched pipe-dream this was.

'Don't worry, my son,' said Enver Araz. 'You have a mother and father and five sisters. Surely one of us can give you a kidney!'

Finally it was arranged that Janet would go and live with Kenan with some other relatives in Istanbul and nurse him through the final crucial months leading up to his exams. The family felt relief at the new arrangement and Kenan felt just as relieved that he would be delivered from all the cooking, and so be restored to the proper Turkish male role of being simply a consumer but not a producer of meals.

Kenan's simple, direct faith over the years since his conversion had also had a profound effect upon the spiritual life of his whole family. Both his parents had come to a more personal faith in Christ through his witness, Janet had been converted as a result of living with other believers in Istanbul some years before, and Kenan's other sisters had been deeply touched by the infectious enthusiasm of his faith. As a family they had begun to trust God too that he would do a miracle in Kenan's life and restore his health.

But in the following months Janet could see Kenan almost visibly fading away before her eyes as he spent his last reserves of energy on the final exams. Some days he could hardly climb the stairs back to the flat and could get to his feet only by pulling himself up using a support.

Then, during one of the exams, Kenan collapsed and went into a coma. He was rushed to hospital, where he pulled out of the coma and was discharged after a few days, immediately going back to his books to prepare for the next exam.

From that day on Kenan had the strongest conviction that he should go to London immediately, otherwise it would be too late. He was dying. This would be his last chance. He could not even wait until his exams were finished; there was no time to lose. During the summer he had been able to make some money by helping friends with a building project. But the money was fast disappearing through doctors' bills. Soon there would not even be enough for the air ticket to England.

But repeatedly Kenan was advised from England that he should *not* go. There was no way he could have a transplant on the National Health Service. It would therefore cost at least £4,000, a sum equivalent at the time to the total income of a Turkish university lecturer during the course of more than three years' work. How could Kenan expect to arrive in England with no financial support? Again the phrase was bandied about that even if he had a transplant, he could only 'exist like a vegetable'.

While cold water was being poured on Kenan's hopes and plans in London, in Istanbul on a warm Tuesday evening during September 1970, Kenan was on his knees praying. Very clearly the Lord once again seemed to be telling him to go to England as soon as possible. First he went round to his closest Christian friends to ask their advice. Gently but firmly they pointed out to Kenan all the

logical reasons why he should *not* go: 'Nothing is arranged
for you at a hospital in London. You don't need to go
immediately. You've waited all this time, so a few more
weeks won't make any difference. Don't worry!'

Kenan was not in fact worried, but the unshakeable
conviction did not leave him that he had to go immediately,
even before his exams were finished. So he did something
that Christians are never supposed to do – he flew in the
teeth of all the good solid advice and decided to go anyway.
It was a decision totally out of character. If anything he was
usually too easily swayed by the advice of others. But this
time things were different; God had spoken and given a
clear assurance that this was his plan, though it would
mean missing the last four papers of his finals, which
would have ensured his graduation.

It was only after Kenan had made the decision to leave
for London that he realised the utter impossibility of ever
doing so. He had no passport and, as a student, one could
only obtain a passport after completion of compulsory
military service, which lasted nearly two years. The only
way around this problem was to obtain a certificate of
unfitness for military duties from an army doctor.

'Oh Lord,' Kenan cried, very weakly but from the bottom
of his heart, 'You see how impossible it is. Please do
something!'

Hardly knowing what he was doing, and barely
conscious, he struggled along to the military headquarters,
pausing to regain strength every few hundred yards. Once
there he asked to see the military doctor. To Kenan's
immense relief the man was in and agreed to see him.

Kenan poured out his heart to the doctor, explaining his
illness and showing medical reports confirming that his
kidneys were rapidly failing. The Turkish doctor listened
patiently. How many sob stories he had heard! How many
men came to him whining, moaning, complaining,
falsifying medical reports, anything so that they could
escape from their dreaded military duties. Some had even
been known to cut off their own trigger fingers so that they

would no longer be eligible. What was this fellow saying?

But somehow as Kenan continued to explain his predicament, this man was deeply touched, and tears came to his eyes as Kenan completed his story.

'Don't worry, my friend,' he said. 'I can see from your face, your whole appearance, that it's true: you are very ill! I'll help you in every way possible to get to England for that operation. By coincidence, today is the day when the military doctors' council meets. Twelve doctors like myself meet to decide which cases should be granted exemption from military service on health grounds. Come along with me and I'll talk to them for you!'

The man was so kind. Kenan breathed a silent prayer of thanksgiving. He remembered the incident in the Ankara court-house some years before and was encouraged. His assurance was strengthened that his Big Father was indeed looking after him: 'Lord, please do the impossible with those doctors this afternoon . . . .' In the afternoon Kenan was taken along to the council of doctors and stood before them feeling very weak. The military doctor who had interviewed him in the morning stood up and began to plead on Kenan's behalf.

'My friends, you see this young man standing before you; you see how weak and pale he is! He needs to go to England to have a kidney transplant, otherwise he'll die very soon. Please, friends, let us accept this case; let us release him from his military service . . . .' And so he continued, on and on and on, and Kenan was amazed to see that he was putting the case with tears in his eyes. The other doctors were very moved, not only seeing Kenan standing there, but also seeing their colleague pleading for him. They knew he had no connections with Kenan and no strings were being pulled.

Kenan could hardly believe his eyes as they signed the paper releasing him from military service. 'Lord, you are wonderful. It seemed so utterly impossible and yet you have done it in one day!'

The following day, Thursday, Kenan went to the passport

office, very conscious that the sands of time were running out. Crowds of people were milling around the office, clutching grubby pieces of paper covered with various stamps and signatures. Some of them had been waiting several days to work through the bureaucracy associated with obtaining a passport. In spite of the way that the Lord had worked things out the day before, Kenan's heart sank within him.

'Lord, you worked such a great miracle yesterday, but how can I get this passport quickly? I feel so ill and weak. I don't think I can go through days of waiting, of being sent from one office to the next. My Big Father, please help me!'

Kenan gradually squirmed his way through the crowd until he finally reached the desk of the woman clerk who began the processing of the application forms. By then it was already past noon.

'Oh dear,' he thought, 'they'll be going off to lunch soon and all this waiting will be wasted.' He started to explain his predicament to the clerk. Again, exactly the same thing happened as the day before. The woman seemed deeply moved as she saw this pallid drooping figure before her.

'Just sit down,' she said. 'I'll get your passport done as quickly as possible. I won't go for my break today; I'll work on getting this finished instead.' So she worked, going from office to office and from desk to desk, processing the application and obtaining all the necessary signatures. She finally came back with his new passport in her hand. Once again Kenan could hardly believe his eyes, as he fingered the vital document. Somehow the past weeks had been so discouraging, culminating with his own closest friends pressing him not to go to London, but now he had seen yet another sign that God was stepping in with his love and power to make possible the impossible.

Kenan almost ran to the Turkish Airlines office, a new surge of hope giving him a fresh burst of physical strength. The next plane to London was leaving the following day, going via Paris. There was room on the flight. Kenan carefully counted out the last of his Turkish lira. There was just enough, and so the ticket was his.

Kenan's friends and relatives were startled to learn of his sudden departure for London the very next day, 9 October. They could not believe that all the arrangements had been made so quickly. A small group of well-wishers came to see him off at the airport, including Janet and Steve and Diane. Some were full of hope, believing that an operation would somehow be possible. The realists thought that they were seeing Kenan for the last time. Steve and Diane were both crying as in turn they kissed him on both cheeks in the traditional farewell. Diane said later that she could feel no flesh left on the cheeks – Kenan had grown so thin.

Soon the Turkish jet rumbled down the runway, and Kenan was off.

8
New Kidney

After a brief stop-over in Paris with one of his uncles who was living there at the time, Kenan flew on to London. On arrival he phoned some friends whose number Steve and Diane had given him and was soon once again in Christian company, with friends who had never met him before but who already knew much of his plight. Though rather surprised at Kenan's sudden and unexpected arrival, they graciously swung into action to see how they could help him.

Events quickly overtook their plans. The very next day, Sunday, Kenan suddenly went into a coma and was rushed to nearby Farnborough Hospital. It was just four days since he had stood before the panel of medical doctors in Istanbul and had been declared unfit for military service.

He was placed immediately in the intensive care unit. It was at once apparent that very high levels of toxin had built up in his blood as a result of almost total failure of both kidneys, and on top of that he had developed pneumonia. Peritoneal dialysis was begun, a process of artificially removing the waste products from the body fluids. It was clear that Kenan was dying and the doctors had little hope for his recovery.

An urgent telephone call went to John, an old friend of Kenan's who spoke good Turkish and who was then in England. He had once lived with Kenan in various batchelor flats in Istanbul. Could he come and help? They urgently needed a translator. John was in Newcastle when he heard the news. During the next few days he had many speaking engagements arranged and was also due to go to Oxford for a degree ceremony to receive his M.A. in law. Cancelling everything, he jumped on the Flying Scotsman express train and headed for London.

Meanwhile, back at Farnborough Hospital, Kenan lay in coma for more than twenty-four hours before his eyes began to flicker and eventually open, focusing on a nurse standing by him. Kenan had no idea where he was or what had happened. The nurse began to explain. Kenan's English was weak, but he knew a few phrases and muttered weakly, 'Praise the Lord!' The nurse was amazed at a Turkish patient suddenly coming out with this expression. 'Oh, are you a Christian?' she said.

Kenan said, 'Of course I'm a Christian. Look, now the Lord's not going to leave me!'

'Oh, praise the Lord!' she exclaimed. 'I'm a Christian too. We've been waiting twenty-four hours for you to open your eyes and I've been praying for you – in fact many have been praying .'

Kenan hardly knew what was going on and was rapidly slipping back into unconsciousness, but found those few words immensely comforting. No, his Big Father had not left him.

As Kenan hovered between life and death, an urgent message went to his uncle in Paris: if he wanted to see his nephew alive, he had better come soon . . . . Kenan's uncle jumped on a plane and came.

Kenan had just come out of his coma when John arrived at the hospital. Kenan had never looked particularly healthy when they had lived together in Istanbul, but now John could hardly recognise him. His face was half-covered with an oxygen mask, there were drips attached to his arms and tubes into his abdomen for the peritoneal dialysis. Electrodes taped to other parts of his body monitored heartbeat and respiration.

There was obviously little that could be done for the moment. So John retired to pray in a guestroom, kindly provided by the hospital. The news of Kenan's critical condition had spread to many who were concerned for God's work in Turkey, and there were many others praying that night in the London area. As there were so very few believers in Turkey, how could it be God's will to allow one to die so young?

The next morning John went in again to see Kenan. If anything, he seemed even worse and again did not recognise John, his vision having been impaired by his condition.

What should they tell Kenan's parents in Turkey? John and the other friends who came to visit agonised over this decision for a long time. The doctors were perfectly plain – if the lad's parents wished to see their son again, alive, they should come quickly, preferably within twenty-four hours. John knew that it was not that easy. Kenan's family hardly had enough money to reach Istanbul, let alone fly to London. He knew the shocking effect a telegram would have on the family at this stage. Having heard that Kenan had left for England with such great hopes, his parents would be crushed by his apparently imminent death and at the same time know that they had no hope of ever seeing their beloved eldest son again. What to do?

In the end, they compromised, sending a telegram to Steve in Istanbul and asking him to show it to another of Kenan's uncles there. The telegram read:

'KENAN NOT EXPECTED TO LIVE MORE THAN A FEW DAYS STOP PLEASE INFORM PARENTS STOP'

The telegram was never forwarded to the Araz family. Those in Istanbul could not face telling them the news either. This was just as well, because two days later another telegram came saying that Kenan was slightly better and might live longer than expected.

It was true. Against all expectations, Kenan was pulling back from death's door. He felt immensely sobered as he gained full consciousness and the realisation of what had happened to him began to sink in. Several doctors explained to him that if he had waited one or two days longer in Turkey he would probably have died. So *that* was why God had given him the deep conviction to come! If the military doctors had not given such a quick reply, or if the woman at the passport office had not been so helpful, or if there had not been enough room on the plane, he would have been delayed; so he would have still been in Istanbul when he went into coma, and Kenan knew that the same equipment was not available there to pull him out. So he would have died. Kenan's faith was strengthened as he realised how many 'ifs' had been involved in his still being alive.

Worth four thousand pounds?

As Kenan gained enough strength to think clearly again, so one over-riding concern dominated his mind. How could he find the money for a kidney transplant? And was it worth the money?

By now Kenan's uncle had arrived from Paris. He found Kenan still totally convinced that a transplant was the only solution and many were the subsequent debates about its feasibility. It was clear that Kenan would only stay alive as long as he was in hospital and close to dialysis facilities. If he went back to Turkey he would soon die. Yet enormous sums were being mentioned for the cost of a transplant – at least several thousand pounds. Furthermore, a good Christian family doctor reiterated his opinion that, taking Kenan's emaciated condition into consideration, there was little hope that he would pull through such a major operation. Even if he did, he explained gravely to Kenan's uncle, 'The very best that we could hope for is that Kenan would live the rest of his life as a vegetable . . . . '

'As a vegetable!' Those words had a powerful effect both on Kenan's closest friends and on his uncle. It was the same phrase that had been used by that German professor. Was it worth spending all that money just so that Kenan could continue to live, but like a vegetable? Perhaps it was simply God's will for him *not* to be healed?

Another telegram was sent to Istanbul. Could the relatives and believers rally round to start raising money for a transplant operation? Everyone knew that Kenan's own family had faced increasing financial difficulties over the past few years. There was simply no way they could pay the bill.

Many Turkish believers gave generously and sacrificially, but the amount raised, which looked so large in Turkish lira, was discouragingly small when converted into English pounds. Kenan's long-time critics in the church in Istanbul gave nothing and one of them wrote to him saying that this kind of operation was 'butchery'.

About this time John had to leave Farnborough Hospital. Who could continue to translate for Kenan's uncle? John remembered that a believer called Jenny, who had lived for some time in Istanbul the previous year, was now living not far from Farnborough. Could she help? At first she was very hesitant since her Turkish was so weak. But, realising the urgency of the situation, she agreed, and after that she started to visit the hospital every day to help Kenan's uncle as he talked to the various doctors and visitors.

Jenny remembered Kenan from her days in Istanbul. At that time she had become very close to one of Kenan's younger sisters, Habibe. As she now went to the hospital night after night with Kenan's uncle, she felt very much the concern of a sister for Kenan. She felt as if she was in Habibe's place. She knew how much Habibe loved her elder brother. Many in London were continuing to pray for Kenan, and Jenny would join them regularly for these prayer times.

One evening Jenny was alone in her room praying. As every night, she prayed that God would heal Kenan. Suddenly out of the stillness she knew that God was speaking to her. Not with a human voice, but as a deep inner conviction:

'Yes, Kenan will get better, and you will marry him.'

It was so clear, and yet so utterly strange, so incredible. In fact, it was so far from anything Jenny had ever contemplated that she could neither take it in nor accept it. She had never been particularly attracted to Kenan. Their personalities were too different to even consider the idea. Besides, she knew something of Kenan's relationship with Anda, and as far as she knew that relationship was continuing.

No, the whole idea was preposterous. Jenny pushed it
out of her mind. Very soon after that she left London to
serve on the Christian training ship *m.v. Logos*, and was
soon many miles away from both England and Kenan.

Meanwhile, Kenan's friends were gradually beginning to
obtain a more accurate picture for him of what a transplant
would involve. By one of those 'coincidences' which
seemed to mark Kenan's whole time in England, one of
John's medical friends from Oxford who had been
receiving his prayer letter from Turkey was now working at
St Mary's Hospital, Paddington. His name was Richard. St
Mary's was one of the leading centres in Britain for kidney
transplant operations. It was through Richard that the link
was made with Professor W S Peart, the director of the
Medical Unit at St Mary's. It emerged that there was a fifty-
fifty chance of a five-year survival following a kidney
transplant. There were plenty of people with transplanted
kidneys who were carrying on fairly normal lives and jobs,
though not particularly energetic ones. Would the fact that
both his kidneys had failed make Kenan's situation worse?
It transpired that in fact an operation would not even be
considered unless both kidneys were almost totally
destroyed, since a person could live perfectly normally
with a single functioning kidney.

One day after John had returned he took Kenan's uncle
to St Mary's to find out exactly how payment for an
operation would be made. The secretary put the hospital's
case very firmly. There had been several instances of
foreigners having operations and then leaving without
paying their bills. The secretary was very sorry, but this
meant that a sizeable deposit had to be made before the
patient even entered the hospital. In the case of a kidney
transplant this sum was £4,000.

£4,000 in advance! They could hardly believe their ears.
It was one thing to accumulate such a sum over a lengthy
period of time – but in advance? It seemed impossible.
Kenan's uncle was almost in tears as they came away from

the interview. John took him for a long walk to try and take his mind off the situation. These two men, one so British-looking and one so very Assyrian, attracted some curious stares as they tramped the streets around Paddington Station, talking loudly in Turkish and gesticulating in their distress.

Many people lost hope when they heard of the financial commitment necessary before Kenan could even be transferred to St Mary's. Kenan was never bereft of visitors, but it was a difficult time for him. Even his closest friends seemed to be willing for him to return to Turkey without an operation and die there! Of course, no one said as much to him directly, but there seemed to Kenan a conspiracy of silence when it came to discussing finances for the operation. Sometimes dark arrows of self-pity pierced his defences, and he would begin to wonder whether people thought he was actually worth as much as £4,000 . . . .

By this time Kenan was out of the intensive care unit and back in a normal ward. He was existing on the most horrible diet of sickly-sweet syrups and some foul powder, all carefully planned to give him the necessary nourishment without overloading his kidneys with waste products. Kenan found the diet nauseating and would often withdraw into fantasies in which his favourite Turkish dishes would drift past him one by one.

The worst part of the daily routine was the injections. Kenan knew logically that these were essential, but found them so painful he could hardly bear them. The nurses felt so much for him; they tried to help, but they had to give the injections. Kenan found that the only way he could bear them was by thinking of his Big Father, and positively praising God. '*Hamd olsun, shukur olsun*' ('Praise the Lord, praise God'), he would shout, as the needle sank into very sensitive parts of his anatomy.

One of the nurses grew curious. By now knowing Kenan a little, she could not believe that he was uttering some powerful Turkish oaths. 'What is it you're saying when I give you the painful injections?' she asked. Kenan explained. Ever after that, whenever that nurse came along with the syringe, she said with an encouraging smile: 'Come on, Kenan – *hamd olsun, shukur olsun!*' Among the nurses Kenan received the nickname Mr Hamd Olsun!

Meanwhile Kenan's uncle could not rest. Emotionally he found himself totally involved with that slim, failing figure lying in the hospital bed, and for the moment his heavy business commitments in Paris were forgotten. This boy was his own nephew! They were from the same village! Kenan's father had helped him so often in the past. In every way he was indebted to the lad. He could not just let him die. But where would the money come from?

For weeks hope dwindled and Kenan seemed to be slipping back again, when suddenly the breakthrough came. A friend in Paris offered a loan of £4,000 to Kenan's uncle, and Kenan's face was wreathed in smiles as his uncle came to give him the good news. The money was on the way! His faith had been vindicated! Two days later the cheque was collected from the American Express office and deposited at St Mary's Hospital. On 13 November 1970, Kenan was transferred there from Farnborough Hospital to prepare for a kidney transplant operation.

His Big Father had not forgotten him.

St Mary's Hospital

St Mary's was superbly equipped to deal with kidney transplants. The first transplant had been performed there in 1959, and up to 1970 more than 180 had been performed. Transplants were no longer in the experimental stage as experience had been gained over the years, particularly in preventing rejection of the grafted organ. A special unit had been established with expert doctors and nurses to deal with transplant patients.

Kenan's condition when he arrived at the private wing of St Mary's was described as 'desperate' by the consulting physician, Dr Hulme. He was barely conscious, sleeping much of the time, and peritoneal dialysis was

recommenced immediately. There was obviously a very
long way to go before Kenan would be fit enough for the
operation.

John's friend, Dr Richard, came to see Kenan straight
away and visited him frequently. The other staff were
amazed. How could this doctor from Oxford and this poor
young student from a tiny Turkish village of which they had
never heard establish such an immediate rapport? It was all
very strange.

One major question remained: who would give Kenan a
kidney? A telegram went off to his family in Midyat telling
them of the planned operation and asking for them to send
information about their blood groups. Knowing little about
all that had happened in the four weeks since Kenan had
flown to England, his family was overjoyed. So their
prayers, too, were being answered!

After much confusion it emerged that Kenan's mother
and his sister, Janet, were the only two in the family whose
blood groups were compatible with Kenan's. Janet was
already in Istanbul. Mrs Araz set out for Istanbul by bus, the
same long thirty-six hour journey that Kenan had first
taken all those years before as he set out so full of life and
hope to start at boarding school. It was a very tearful
goodbye as she bade her final farewells to Enver, to
Kenan's sisters, and to Haluk, Kenan's little brother, who
was then just five years old. There was only a dim
awareness of what a kidney transplant involved. Some
thought that Mrs Araz was sacrificing her life for her son,
for how could someone lose a kidney and still live?

On arrival in Istanbul it became apparent that there was
not enough money available for the flight to London. But it
so happened that some friends of Kenan who had been
working in Turkey had just decided to return to England.
They had room for one or two more people in their old
converted ambulance. Would Mrs Araz like to come along?
Up until then it had been assumed that Kenan's mother
would travel alone. Two places! Janet jumped at the
opportunity to go too and help look after her mother. So it

was agreed, and within a few days of arriving in Istanbul Janet and Mrs Araz found themselves bumping along the long, boring main road through Bulgaria and Yugoslavia, wedged in on every side by furniture in a decrepit old ambulance that seemed to be held together by a mixture of faith and string.

Many were the delays experienced on that long and frustrating journey as the ambulance itself seemed to be in the throes of some terminal illness. Tempers were becoming not a little frayed when the engine finally gave up the ghost on a German *autobahn*. Once again they were stranded and it was several more days before kind friends provided money so that the two women could continue by air to London.

At London Airport there were more delays. They had come to England without entry visas and the immigration authorities, viewing them as illegal immigrants, tried to explain that they would be placed on a plane back to Istanbul. Mrs Araz gesticulated in voluble Syriac, breaking into Arabic and Turkish during moments of particular excitement, but the officials were not impressed. Janet knew the word 'kidney' in English and used it frequently, but this seemed only to add to the confusion. Finally a translator came. A phone call was made to St Mary's to check the story, and the two soon found themselves passing through customs.

It was a triumphant moment when Kenan's mother and sister walked through the door of his room in St Mary's on a cold wet day in December – however, a great shock awaited Mrs Araz. The last time she had seen her son had been the previous summer. She knew he had been very ill, but the gaunt pale face with dark sunken eyes that faced her as she came into the room could surely not be Kenan!

It was a time when Kenan's vision was much impaired, and at first he did not recognise who had come. But as soon as Mrs Araz gathered up his frail body in a big hug, tears began to fill Kenan's eyes and he realised once more the faithfulness of his Big Father.

'And who is this other person with you?' he asked.

'Oh Kenan, I'm Janet. Your sister Janet!' she cried.

Kenan was overjoyed. He had never expected to see his sister here as well. Now everything would surely turn out all right.

For Kenan's mother, especially, it was extremely hard to adjust to their new life in London. She had rarely left Midyat and even then it had only been to travel to nearby towns. Journeying to Istanbul had been like going to another country, but now suddenly to be plunged into the middle of London was almost too much.

Mrs Araz and Janet moved into an hotel opposite the hospital. The first night, Kenan's mother could not sleep. Everything was so strange, and images of the gaunt, pale face kept swimming before her eyes. Perhaps her son would die before she could even give her kidney.

Now that the hospital authorities knew that a potential kidney donor was present, they concentrated their efforts on preparing Kenan for the big operation, changing treatment from peritoneal dialysis to a proper kidney machine. There were only a few such machines in the hospital at the time, as each was extremely costly, though in continual use. Five nights a week Kenan would be 'plugged in' to have his blood cleaned out. At the commencement of the treatment a shunt was inserted into his arm, connecting an artery to a vein. When dialysis began, the shunt tubes were disconnected and linked to the machine, so that his blood would be by-passed through the machine and thus detoxified.

At the end of each session Kenan felt emotionally drained. He knew that his life depended on that single column of blood as it passed through the machine. One little blood clot and he could be finished. In fact on two occasions he almost died while undergoing dialysis. The nurse sitting with him did not notice the blood clot in the tube until it was almost too late.

Meanwhile, exhaustive tests were being carried out on Janet and Mrs Araz as well to find out who should be the

donor. The renal tissues of Kenan's mother matched better
with his than did those of his sister, so Mrs Araz was chosen
to be the donor. Despite having given birth to ten children,
she was a healthy wiry forty-six year old, the pure air and
hard work of life in Midyat having kept her fit throughout
the years.

There was one problem – did she really understand what
was involved in giving one of her kidneys? There had been
too many cases of emotional pressure being put on
potential donors, especially when they were close
relatives. The doctor called Mrs Araz for a consultation,
with Dale to translate. He explained that if she changed her
mind about being the donor he could always tell Kenan and
the other family members that her kidney was not suitable,
so she would not lose face and would be under no pressure.

Dale turned to Mrs Araz and asked her in Turkish if she
truly wanted to give one of her kidneys to Kenan. Did she
fully realise the gravity of such an operation?

Oh Dale,' she burst out, 'the doctors keep on asking me
whether I want to give my kidney. Of course I want to give
it! I want Kenan to live. I don't want him to die! Please tell
them I want to give it. In fact, if they want, I can give both
my kidneys!'

The doctors were touched; there was no doubting the
woman's sincerity. Later it emerged that Mrs Araz had
originally thought that she would probably die when she
gave her kidney. She had set out on the long journey from
Midyat expecting to face death so that her son could live.

It was also found at St Mary's that one of her kidneys was
larger than the other – not an unusual occurrence. 'Please
take the big one for Kenan!' pleaded Mrs Araz. The doctors
assured her that the small one would be perfectly adequate.

While the doctors and nurses of St Mary's were
impressed by the joyful willingness of both Mrs Araz and
Janet to donate their kidneys, they were truly amazed at the
enormous numbers of visitors who came to see Kenan
from the beginning of his stay there. Who was this young
Turk? All the world seemed to know him. The matron was

very puzzled. Perhaps he was very rich and famous? In the end she decided it would be best to let Kenan entertain his friends in the small lounge just along from the main ward. Would matron mind if they sang hymns and prayed in the small lounge? No, came the answer, so long as it did not disturb the other patients.

On his better days the lounge was crowded with visitors, and Kenan would sit stately in their midst, pyjama-clad. He would laugh and joke freely, with his 'dialytic' arm carefully resting on one knee. A strong smell of Turkish coffee would waft down the corridor, Kenan's only disappointment being that he could never drink it since his fluid in-take was carefully controlled. Then would come some hymn singing, in Turkish or English or both, depending on the mixture of visitors on that particular day. Afterwards the room would suddenly grow quiet as, heads bowed, each one prayed for Kenan and for the tiny suffering Church in Turkey.

Many of Kenan's visitors were people he had never met before, people who had a concern to pray for Turkey and had heard that he was in St Mary's. Others were old friends of John from Oxford, where there had been a strong prayer interest in Turkey for many years. Many went to St Mary's with the idea of encouraging a sick patient and came away themselves uplifted by Kenan's infectious faith.

From his earliest days at St Mary's Kenan made no secret of the fact that he was a Christian. He had a natural outgoing way of witnessing that quickly won the hearts of his listeners. Being from the Middle East gave many openings, as most people seemed to be under the impression that Turkey resembled Saudi Arabia, or had Muslim sheikhs galloping their camels across endless sand dunes; the news that there were Christians there came as something of a surprise.

Kenan witnessed freely to everyone he met: doctors, nurses, patients and visitors. Several Arabs who were in the hospital heard the gospel for the first time. Many times

Kenan witnessed to an English patient who was also
waiting for a kidney transplant. Some years later when
Kenan revisited St Mary's he learned that this man had
become a Christian.

On some days Kenan felt terrible. He could hardly
concentrate enough to pray, let alone witnes to anyone.
The illness would suck him into a vortex of despair. He
would get fed up with the hospital and sometimes shout at
Janet. After these episodes he would feel full of remorse,
thinking that it spoiled his whole witness in the hospital.
But a visitor reminded him that God knew all about his
bodily frailty and weaknesses. He pointed out that Kenan
could not expect his emotions to remain unaffected by his
physical state. Being a true follower of Christ was not a
question of being super-human, but of being a normal
person who had learned to live at the foot of the cross.
Kenan felt very reassured by these words.

It was a great relief, however, when a date was finally
fixed for the transplant operation. It was to be on 22
December. This was a time when the wards were festooned
with Christmas trees and paper chains. Several people
joked that Mrs Araz could hardly give a better present than
one of her own kidneys!

The word was passed around the various prayer groups
and churches that had been praying continually for Kenan
since he arrived in England. Telegrams were sent to
Turkey. A great wave of prayer went up on the evening
before the operation. Kenan felt tremendously elated; at
last the great day had come! But that very evening he felt a
curious pain in his leg. Professor Peart came to examine
him. The time was nine o'clock. At first the Professor said
nothing, but then Kenan noticed him huddled with the
other doctors, discussing in low voices. His heart began to
sink. Had something gone wrong? Professor Peart came
back. He was very sorry to inform Kenan that unfortunately
a blood clot had formed in his leg and moved to his lungs.
Under the circumstances it would be impossible to
perform the operation. It would actually require three

months before Kenan would be healthy enough to try again.

The sense of anticlimax was enormous. Everything in Kenan had been built up for that day. Had his Big Father made a mistake? No, it was impossible. He knew that God did not make mistakes. But why had he allowed this to happen?

Dr Richard came in. He was also very upset and was almost in tears like Kenan. 'Don't worry,' he said. 'Maybe it's better for you. The Lord surely has his purpose in it. Come on. Don't be sad. Let's pray.'

Kenan prayed, but it took him a long time to settle that night. Again he talked with Dr Richard. Could he not persuade the other doctors to change their minds? Dr Richard laughed. No, that was not his job.

'Lord, give me patience!'

Kenan had another worry on his mind. How could his mother and Janet possibly live another three months in that expensive hotel? And how could he afford to lie another three months in the private wing of St Mary's? He had already been there for six weeks, and the bill was surely mounting. Kenan's uncle from Paris had said he would meet the bills, but this situation could not go on forever.

The next day Kenan phoned Dale (who was then living in Austria) and told him what had happened. Years of living in the Middle East had taught Dale to be flexible in his arrangements. 'Don't worry, Kenan,' he said. 'I can't promise to do much, but I'll come immediately.'

The next day Dale arrived at St Mary's. Another visitor that day was Hristo, Kenan's old friend from Istanbul days who was now living in London. Together with Mrs Araz, they all sat on Kenan's bed, thinking and praying about what they could do to help. Then Hristo suddenly remembered that his church had a small house lying vacant in Streatham, South London. It was a bit damp and was

unfurnished, he explained, but would they like to use it?
(No charge would be made for the rent!) Kenan jumped at
the idea. His Big Father had certainly not forgotten them!

Then there was another piece of good news. The doctors
informed Kenan that it was now no longer necessary for
him to stay in hospital. Although his kidneys were not
functional at this stage, he would be kept alive by coming
for dialysis on the artificial kidney machine at St Mary's
twice a week. Was there anywhere he could stay? The
doctors were amazed when Kenan told them about the
rent-free house that had just been provided for them. Rent-
free accommodation near central London . . . why, that was
the ideal situation. But how could this family from a little
Turkish village have achieved such a thing! Kenan tried to
explain, but it was too hard for them to understand how
their big Father provides for his children.

So the three of them moved into their new home.
However, the months that followed were certainly not
easy, despite the help of many local Christians. They all
knew that Kenan's life hung on a thread. Mrs Araz always
had an inner fear that Kenan would die before being
healthy enough for a transplant. Janet also was terrified of
the possibility of a clot forming in the shunt in Kenan's arm,
knowing from her time at St Mary's that this could be fatal.
During that whole period she found herself sleeping very
fitfully, waking every few minutes to check the shunt. One
cold night in January she could not sleep at all, and then it
happened! The blood clotted. Janet did not know what to
do. Hurriedly pulling her coat over her nightdress, she
staggered out into the street with Kenan slung across her
back. Her English was extremely limited, and she had no
idea how to use a public telephone (there being no phone in
the house), nor how to find a taxi. Suddenly she spied a
couple coming down the road towards them. She stopped
them, waving frantically; she was by then very close to
tears. Kenan kept saying, 'Praise the Lord! Praise the Lord!'
Janet showed them Kenan's arm and shouted 'Kidney!
Kidney! Kidney no good! Taxi! Taxi!'

Now it so happened that Janet had encountered two phlegmatic and kind-hearted members of the British public of a breed that one would not generally expect to be at large on the streets of Streatham at one o'clock in the morning. The man leaped into action. 'You stay with them, my dear,' he said to his wife, and ran off to fetch a taxi. Returning breathlessly with a taxi a few minutes later, he insisted on paying the fare. Then the couple waved goodbye and they never met again. Kenan always felt that they were like angels sent by God specially to help them on that cold dark January night.

Kenan became more and more convinced that God had some very special plan yet to reveal to him. How many times God had kept him alive when he could so easily have died!

New kidney

The long months dragged by. A new date was set for the transplant: 30 March, 1971. This time, surely, nothing could prevent it from actually taking place!

Kenan knew that he could well die during the long and risky operation. Someone had told him, perhaps unwisely, that for a person in his physical state there was only a twenty per cent chance of surviving the operation – let alone the after-effects! Only twenty per cent? Kenan would not believe it. Anyway, his Big Father was quite capable of dealing with such slim odds. Notwithstanding, Kenan was a realist and did not play down the seriousness of its implications.

Shortly before it began he had a long talk about it with his sister. 'Look, Janet,' he said, 'you must promise me that if I die during this operation, there mustn't be that terrible weeping and wailing and mourning that normally happens in Midyat when someone dies. I certainly don't want you to wear black clothes for years. You must be happy for me. You know where I'm going. You'll know I'll be so happy . . . .'

Janet never forgot those words.

The news about Kenan's forthcoming transplant spread far and wide. Several people wrote and said that they would fast and pray for Kenan throughout the day of the operation. Back in Midyat, Kenan's three younger sisters decided to completely abstain from food and water for the last three days of March.

Cards, letters and telegrams began to flood into the hospital, from Turkey, India and the United States, as well as from many prayer partners and well-wishers in England. Again the doctors and nurses were mystified. Many rich and famous people came to St Mary's for treatment, but hardly anyone they could remember had received so much mail.

Kenan and his mother were admitted to St Mary's on 30 March. This time there were no last-minute hitches. Kenan seemed to be as medically ready as he ever would be for such an operation. Dr Richard prayed in English with Mrs Araz while she lay on the trolley before being wheeled into the operating theatre. She smiled and made a one-way sign to heaven as the doors swung open and she was wheeled inside. It was four o'clock in the afternoon.

The journey from the little village of Midyat to the operating tables of a famous London hospital had been very long indeed . . . .

Meanwhile Kenan was being prepared in another operating theatre down the corridor for the much longer operation by which the blood supply to his own diseased kidneys would be tied off, then the circulation prepared so that the blood supply would filter through the new kidney, to be supplied by his mother.

As Kenan was wheeled into the ante-room where he would be prepared for the operation, he suddenly experienced the most wonderful joy. Never in his whole life had he felt such joy pouring into his life. It was so unexpected, so overwhelming, that he started to praise the Lord.

'*Hamd olsun! Shukur olsun!*' he shouted, and started to sing hymns in Turkish to praise his Big Father. The nurse rushed over to him. She had seen many different reactions before in the ante-room to the operating theatre. Some patients came in crying and weeping, others came in white-faced, afraid to even talk or look at the nurses. But she had never seen anything like this! Had the boy become hysterical?

'Kenan, are you all right? What's the matter? Don't you realise how serious this operation is?'

'Yes, I do, but I'm so happy. You see, the thing is I *know* that if I die tonight I'm going to live with Jesus Christ forever. And if I live – well, I'll live for him!'

The nurse shook her head. She still could not understand what was happening. 'He must be crazy,' she thought. She fetched the doctor, while Kenan continued to praise the Lord loudly in Turkish. Kenan repeated his explanation to the doctor, who shook his head and gave a broad smile. 'Well,' he said, 'there's only one thing that can stop this singing!' and duly proceeded to administer the anaesthetic to Kenan. And it did stop the joy and the singing, but only for a few hours!

Janet went into a room nearby. She had already been fasting for twenty-four hours, but it was difficult to concentrate on praying. A Christian nurse came to sit with her. Janet kept thinking of cold sharp scalpels, and then her mind would drift to Midyat, and she wondered what the family was doing. In fact they were restless too, wandering about the house, waiting for the telephone to ring. A strong warm wind from the Syrian deserts in the south blew across the rolling hills, bringing down the remains of the almond blossoms and rattling the window panes.

Every now and then Dr Richard would pop his head around the door to give Janet the latest news. Soon after one of the kidneys had been removed from Mrs Araz he came in very excited. 'It's a beaut!' he said. 'I heard the doctors raving over it's marvellous colour. They were saying it's more like the kidney of a young girl than of a woman aged forty-six!'

The kidney was carefully transported to the nearby

theatre where another team off doctors was working on Kenan. Now came the trickiest part of the operation – to insert the new kidney into his body, with all the new connections correctly made. Since Kenan's own diseased kidneys would be left where they were, he would soon be a man with three kidneys.

By eight o'clock that evening, with the last stitches completed, the long operation was finally over, and Kenan was transferred to the recovery room. The whole procedure had lasted four long hours. For Janet it seemed like an eternity. She knew that there was little chance of seeing Kenan face to face for some days. The doctors had told her that he would probably spend several days in a totally sterile room after the operation so that he would not be exposed to infection. But at least she could wait for her mother to wake up.

Meanwhile, Kenan was gradually pulling out of the anaesthetic. He felt as if he was flowing along a very long tunnel, and there at the end was a small circle of light that gradually grew larger as he drifted towards it. There was a noise. Someone was talking loudly. Dr Richard, still in theatre mask and gown, was sitting on the bed beside him, very excited, prodding Kenan to try and rouse him.

'Wake up, brother, wake up. Praise the Lord, your new kidney is working very well. Your kidney is working! Praise the Lord! Look!'

As Kenan slowly opened his eyes, he saw a sight that was to be forever imprinted on his mind. Tubes were protruding from his body, and on each side of his bed he saw a nurse solemnly standing with a bottle in her hands. Slowly but steadily the bottles were filling up with urine. This sight, normally very unpleasant and unmentionable, was now to Kenan the most wonderful sight in the world. He lay there watching in fascinated silence. Not only had he survived the operation, but the new kidney was actually working!

Dr Richard went down to see Janet. 'Come quickly if you want to see a miracle,' he said. 'Kenan's kidney is working!' As the operation had gone so well, it had been decided that there was no need for Kenan to go into isolation. So Janet went to the special renal unit where Kenan had been taken after the operation. At the door she hesitated. Despite all she had been through, she was still squeamish, and hated the sight of blood and suffering. What was she going to see?

To Janet's amazement Kenan was sitting up in bed between the bottles that were still filling up with urine, looking as pleased as Punch, and around him scurried doctors and nurses looking equally pleased with themselves. An enormous wave of relief swept over her. Now she could relax at last. After another good look at this extraordinary sight, it was clear that there was nothing more to be done, so Dr Richard took her back to Streatham.

Back at St Mary's a nurse bent over Kenan before he finally settled for the night. Was there anything he needed? Kenan was fighting extremely hard to take everything in. Was it really true that he could be normal again? For so long now his fluid in-take had been severely restricted. Sometimes he had gone almost mad with thirst and he had long applied a special cream to his lips every day to prevent them from cracking.

'Do you think . . . possible . . . I could have a glass of water?'

The nurse soon returned with a glass, and lifted it gently to Kenan's lips. As he swallowed the cool liquid in large gulps, it seemed to him as if he was consuming heavenly nectar straight from Paradise itself.

That night Janet was so excited that she could hardly sleep. The next morning she was up with the sun, and out to the shops as soon as they began to open. She was determined to buy every food possible that Kenan had been denied during the previous years of regimented diets. Soon she was buying vast quantities of grapes, apples and oranges, and masses of other delicacies. Then she bought him socks, a nice belt and a large box of chocolates. Finally she bought a very expensive shirt, white with elaborate embroidery down the front, and staggered to the hospital with her prizes. She opened the door of Kenan's room to find him sitting up in bed eating an enormous English breakfast. 'Look,' he said, patting his stomach gently, 'I've been eating eggs and bacon, and I just ate an orange too!' Kenan laughed so much when he saw Janet laden with all the other goodies that it began to hurt his stitches. When Dr Richard saw the shirt, he said, 'Kenan, what a beautiful shirt! This is like a wedding shirt! You must keep it for your wedding!' This was intended as a joke, but all at once Kenan decided not to wear it. And, in the end, he did keep it for his wedding!

As the news of the successful operation spread, flowers and telegrams of congratulation began to pour in from all over the world. Two large bunches of flowers came from Dr Francis Schaeffer, who had never forgotten Kenan's visit to L'Abri in Switzerland a few summers before. After many frustrating hours, Enver Araz managed to get through on the phone from Midyat to express his delight.

The first day after the operation the professor in charge came to see Kenan. 'You're a very lucky man,' he said. 'In the ten years we've been performing transplants, yours is the most successful we've ever done. Usually it takes time for a new kidney to work – at least a couple of hours; sometimes not until the next day, and often longer. But in your case the kidney was functional within an hour of the operation being finished. It's like a miracle! I can't understand it.'

Kenan smiled and pointed up to heaven, saying, 'Oh, I can. My Big Father did it!' The professor looked at him long and hard, and finally nodded thoughtfully. 'Well,' he said, 'maybe you're right.'

One of the first people in London to hear about the successful operation was Hristo. He hurried to St Mary's rather apprehensively. Like Janet he was uncertain of what he would see; he had also been told that Kenan would have to stay in a sterile room and be looked at through a glass window. Hristo was directed down a corridor towards the recovery room. Suddenly he heard singing and laughter, and as he turned the corner he saw Kenan sitting up in bed as

large as life! Hristo was so suddenly overwhelmed at the
goodness of God, that there in the middle of the hospital,
with all the nurses, doctors and patients sitting around,
he lifted up his arms to heaven and shouted praises to God
in Turkish at the top of his voice! The hospital personnel
had by now become used to the eccentricities of Kenan's
various visitors and took this latest outburst in their stride.

'Lord, show me what to do!'

As Kenan gradually gained strength, helped by daily visits
to the physiotherapist, so more people began to talk to him
about his future. 'You'll be able to finish your studies as an
engineer now,' they said. 'That's a good career – plenty of
opportunities, plenty of money. Of course you'll be able to
stay in England now. The doctors can give you a special letter so that you can obtain permanent residence, and you
could be near the hospital for check-ups. Life will be easy
from now on.'

Kenan did not say very much as people kept talking. But
in his heart he knew one thing – he had made a very serious
promise to his Big Father. He remembered the joy he had
experienced just before the operation and the reason for
that joy; that if he died that night he would go to live forever
with Jesus Christ, and that if he lived, then he would live for
him. *He would live for him.* Yes, it was a serious vow that
he had made to God. Now, more than ever before, God
must come first in every part of his life – in where he should
live, in what job he should take and whom, if anyone, he
should marry.

Of course it would be nice to go on living in England! He
had so many friends there now. Life was so much easier
than living in Turkey with its tumultuous politics, unpre-
dictable economy and opposition to Christian witness.
Kenan was often tempted as he lay in bed, dreaming of a
quiet house in suburbia, with roses in the front garden and
an English wife welcoming him home after a hard day's
work at the office. But deep down he knew it could never

be like that. He knew that his Big Father wanted him to go
back and live in Turkey. So few there had heard that his Big
Father was truly alive and had a personal love for them.

'Lord, show me what to do,' Kenan would pray almost
daily. He had plenty of time to think and pray through those
remaining months in hospital.

One matter that he often prayed about was the £4,000
debt to his uncle. How was he ever going to refund such an
enormous sum? Kenan had long since decided that once he
had returned to Turkey and completed his diploma he
would pay it back by his own hard work as an engineer. But
once he had made this decision, something very strange
had started to happen. Even before the operation, gifts had
started to arrive. There were small gifts and big gifts, in dol-
lars, sterling, and Turkish lira; all kinds of currencies. Many
were anonymous. Kenan was constantly amazed at the
greatness of his heavenly Father in providing for his children's needs. One day after the transplant an anonymous
cheque for $1,000 arrived. Kenan never found out from
whom it came. No appeals of any kind had been made and
Kenan himself never asked for money. But as people had
started praying, God had placed the financial need upon
their hearts.

On 12 June, 1971, Kenan was finally discharged from St
Mary's and allowed to go and live with his mother and Janet
in their house in Streatham. Mrs Araz was so happy to see
him home again safely that she performed the *kileli*, much
to the curiosity of the neighbours!

With Kenan's discharge from hospital came the day of financial reckoning. Kenan was surprised on receiving the
final bill to find that it only came to £3,500, and the balance
of £500 from the £4,000 deposit was returned to him. On
studying the financial details he found that some of the
doctors and hospital staff had not charged for certain of
their services, and the professor had decided not to charge
any fees for the operation on Mrs Araz. Somehow Kenan
had built such happy relationships with the staff of the hospital over his months there that everyone wanted to make

his final bill as small as possible.

The kindness of all those at St Mary's impressed Kenan greatly, but he was truly amazed when he came to add up all the gifts that he had received while in England. The amount was almost precisely what he needed to pay his debt to his uncle, and within days he was able to send the full amount off to Paris. Indeed God had been very good! Kenan felt so relieved. Now when he went back to Turkey he could start his life again without the great burden of a debt around his neck. During the weeks and months after coming out of hospital, Kenan was euphorically happy, but still there was the underlying concern about what was going on inside him. He knew that often new kidneys were rejected by the body within the first few months after the transplant. Every day he had to take pills that helped to suppress his body's immune system, so lessening the chance of the body rejecting the kidney. At the beginning he also had to go to St Mary's three times a week for checkups. As the weeks went by and the kidney continued to function normally, so Kenan was gradually able to relax more. He always knew that his mother's kidney would be the best!

Return to health

Convalescence was helped by the happy atmosphere in the little household in Streatham. A constant stream of visitors would drop by to chat and sip glasses of sweet Turkish tea. Around the corner lived the Araz's great friends, Mr and Mrs Wooderson, whose own house seemed to be perpetually full of people. Sunday lunch at their home was a great occasion, as all kinds of people in the neighbourhood would be invited in, including many lonely overseas students. The Woodersons had a simple, direct, cheery faith that was very similar to Kenan's, and when the Araz family went to visit there they were somehow reminded of their home back in Midyat.

Having so many friends scattered over Britain, the

Woodersons were adept at arranging cheap holidays for
their friends in various faraway places. When Kenan had
gained some strength, they took him off for a holiday in a
tiny village in the wilds of Wales. It was arranged that Al, a
good friend of Kenan's who had also worked in Turkey for
a while, would join them later.

On the evening Al was due to arrive, they went down to
meet his train, but happened to arrive too late. It was after
midnight and a deathly stillness lay over the village and the
surrounding hills. It was obvious that Al had given up waiting and had gone off to look for them. How to find him?
Without saying a word, Kenan cupped his hands and let out
the cry from the minaret: '*Allah akbaaaaaar* . . . !' The long
wailing cry in Arabic ('God is great!') echoed across the val-
ley. It was certainly the first and possibly the last time that
the Muslim call to prayer had been proclaimed so clearly in
this particular corner of Wales. Windows went up, owls
screeched and not a few slumbering Welsh miners stirred
uneasily in their beds but, sure enough, a few seconds later
Al's answering call to prayer came back from a telephone
kiosk up the road. A few minutes later they were together.

Kenan's sense of humour was ever ready for expression.
Once he was attending a Christian conference. Standing in
line with a tray one mealtime, edging his way towards
where the food was being doled out, Kenan recognised the
Christian doctor who had been so pessimistic about his
condition, standing right in front of him. This was the very
man who had stated that Kenan would live the rest of his
life as a vegetable even if he pulled through a transplant operation. Kenan engaged him in polite conversation. It soon
became obvious that the good doctor did not recognise
him. Kenan waited until the plates were well-laden with
food, and then said casually: 'Well, don't you recognise
me?'

Kenan explained who he was. The doctor was so amazed
that he dropped his plate!

As Kenan gained strength, there was one weekly activity
that he would never miss. He loved to go with an evangelis-

tic team up to Speakers' Corner in Hyde Park and preach and witness to the crowds that gathered there throughout the summer months. Such freedom to proclaim Christ in the open air thrilled Kenan very much. He used to chide his British Christian friends: 'You don't know how lucky you are! In Turkey we have a constitution that guarantees the freedom to preach the gospel in the open air, but if you actually do it you'll either be shot at by fanatics or put in prison by the police. Here you seem to have no constitution at all, yet you can preach quite freely!'

Kenan could never understand why Christians did not use the enormous freedom and opportunities that they had.

People of many nationalities and all kinds of backgrounds were reached with the gospel in this way, including many Muslims. Those on the team would take it in turns to get up on the soapbox and give testimonies. Kenan revelled in these opportunities. Why, he could reach more Muslims in an open way here than he could back in Turkey! He would look down on the sea of faces of varied complexions – some hostile, some curious, some amused – and then launch into his testimony:

'Have you ever heard of a man with three kidneys?' he would begin, and then go on to explain how God had given him not only a new lease of physical life with his new kidney, but a whole new spiritual life through a personal relationship with Jesus Christ.

The crowd always used to swell slightly when Kenan stepped up on the soapbox. A Turkish Christian preaching the gospel in Hyde Park was not something people could see every day of the week. Once a big brawny man at the back of the crowd started heckling Kenan: 'I'm God!' he roared.

'You can't be God', shouted Kenan. 'God is my Father. He's very big. He's bigger than you!'

'How big is he then?' yelled the brawny man.

Kenan flung his arms out wide and stretched them as far as he could: 'He's as big as this and bigger!'

The crowd laughed, the heckler gave up, and Kenan carried on with his testimony.

What about Jenny?

The long summer months passed in a whirl of visits, holidays, making friends, going to Christian conferences and joining in various forms of evangelistic outreach. But as Kenan looked forward more and more to returning to Turkey, there was one great ache in his heart, one great need that began to occupy his thoughts more and more. How and where was he going to find a Christian wife?

Kenan knew that the number of believing girls in Turkey was tiny – at that time they could almost be counted on the fingers of one hand. Christian girls there with the same kind of interests and background as he had were almost non-existent. And what would people say about his medical condition? Kenan knew how people's minds would work; they would not understand him having an extra kidney. They would say to themselves: 'This man's going to die soon. I can't let my daughter marry him – she might soon be left a widow!'

Kenan knew that medically speaking, they could be right. There was always the chance that his kidney might be rejected. It was like a sword of Damocles hanging over his life. How could he possibly find a wife who could cope with that kind of pressure?

When Dale came back to England, Kenan shared his need with him. Kenan had known Dale since the earliest days when he had become a Christian. He had learned so much from Dale's life. How many times they had talked and laughed and prayed together. Kenan valued Dale's opinion very highly, and Dale never gave careless or shallow advice. Often Kenan would ask, 'Dale, what do you advise in this situation?', and Dale would nod his head up and down like a wise old owl and say, 'Well, let's pray about it.'

It was not that he did not want to help, but rather he wanted to be sure of what God's will was for the situation before he spoke.

So it was that on this September day in 1971, Kenan was talking to Dale about his future. Dale was listening and nodding wisely, when he suddenly stopped and said, seemingly out of the blue: 'Kenan, what do you think about Jenny?'

Kenan stopped. 'Jenny?' He could hardly remember who Jenny was. Then he remembered – she was the girl who had spent some time in Istanbul and had been so close to his sister, Habibe. He remembered her coming to the Turkish fellowship in Istanbul, but he could not remember having spoken to her during that time. He remembered, anyhow, that he had been very reluctant to practise his faltering English then, and Jenny did not speak much Turkish. Oh, and was she not the girl who had come to help his uncle in Farnborough Hospital? Kenan vaguely remembered Jenny coming, but he had been so ill then that he certainly could not remember when he had talked to her.

Kenan respected Dale's opinions, but this suggestion certainly seemed a bit strange. Why, he hardly knew the girl! When he arrived back at Streatham that day, Kenan suddenly remembered that Jenny had sent him a 'get-well' card soon after she had left England. Thinking that the card might give him a clue, he started sorting through the hundreds of cards, letters and telegrams that had poured in over the last year in England. Finally he found two small cards that Jenny had sent, expressed in rather bad Turkish. There was nothing special about them. They were similar to hundreds of others that had arrived during his months in hospital. There was certainly nothing to suggest that Jenny herself had any personal interest in him . . . .

Kenan pushed the idea from his mind. A few weeks later he met up with his old friend John. John was about to get married to a Spanish girl who had also gone to Turkey with the specific aim of sharing her faith. Kenan was always amazed that God should send witnesses of so many different nationalities. There was no way that a Turk could say that Christianity was an American or English religion.

Now John had invited Kenan to be best man at his wedding. This in itself tickled Kenan's sense of humour, but it moved him as well. What unity there was in the family of God! Here was he, a believer from a tiny town in eastern Turkey, the name of which he was sure none of the wedding guests had ever heard, dressed up in coat and tails at a posh reception and acting as best man for this quiet, unassuming Oxford graduate to whom God had drawn him so close.

It seemed to Kenan almost as if God had his own special heavenly sense of humour, and delighted to use his kingdom to turn upside down the normal traditions of men, cutting across every barrier of race and nationality as he did so.

The night before the wedding Kenan and John were sharing a room. John was tossing to and fro restlessly. How could anyone expect a man to sleep on such a night! Kenan was cheerfully trying out his repertoire of jokes to see which ones would be most suitable for his speech the following day. Then, not unnaturally, the conversation drifted around to marriage. Unexpectedly, John suddenly said:

'Have you ever thought about Jenny?'

Kenan could not believe his ears. First Dale, now John, were suggesting the same person! Now *he* was the one who could not sleep that night! Could his Big Father be saying something to him? Was Jenny really the one?

From that day on, Kenan began to pray more seriously: 'Father, if you are showing Jenny to me, then please work it out.' In fact he even started praying that he would somehow meet her on his forthcoming trip back to Turkey, though Kenan hardly knew where she was. He knew that she had left England the previous autumn to work on the gospel ship *m.v. Logos*. He had heard from others that the ship was now in India. Where she would be next he had no idea. At the same time Kenan started praying that, if Jenny was the one for him, both their families *and* his many Christian friends back in Turkey would look favourably on the marriage. This was quite a list of requests for someone who hardly knew who Jenny was!

By October the doctors began to tell Kenan that he was

now fit enough to go and visit his family and friends for a short time, as long as he then returned to London for a further check-up. After many delays Kenan and his mother finally flew off to Istanbul, leaving Janet behind in England to complete treatment of a long-term eye problem that had been diagnosed during her stay in London and necessitated an operation.

It was just fourteen months since Kenan had arrived in England pale, thin, undernourished and on the point of death. Now he was returning to Turkey a different person – full cheeks back to their normal healthy brown, if anything a little overweight, with a new kidney that was, according to the doctors' report 'working like clockwork'.

As the plane circled down over the Marmara Sea, and the serpentine contours of the Bosphorous came into view dividing the wooded hills of Europe and Asia on either side, Kenan felt a sudden surge of joy. What miracles God had done to bring him back safely to the land he loved!

9
Back to Turkey

For the tiny church in Istanbul, as for Kenan's many other friends and relatives, it was as if Kenan had returned from the dead when he stepped from the plane at Istanbul Airport with a broad, triumphant smile on his face on that wet and blustery day in late November 1971.

A year earlier they had watched Kenan fading away before their eyes. Now here he was plump and cheerful, full of *hamd olsuns* as he kissed and embraced those who had come to meet him.

Steve and Diane and their family were overjoyed. They had been involved perhaps most closely with Kenan in the years leading up to the transplant. They knew all the trials and disappointments he had been through. The last time they had seen him was at that tearful farewell as he had set out for London more than a year ago. Now he was so bouncy and exuberant that they found it difficult to keep up with him!

Kenan set off round Istanbul to visit all his friends and relatives, using every opportunity possible to tell them what his Big Father had done for him. Assyrians, Greeks, Armenians, Muslim Turks . . . . Kenan witnessed freely to all of them. Nothing could stop him sharing what God had done.

Travelling in buses, *dolmushes* and taxis, Kenan would start chatting with the person sitting next to him. Then, giving his big flashing smile, he would ask them: 'Have you ever talked to a man with three kidneys?' By the time the person had recovered himself sufficiently to shake his head in disbelief, Kenan would already be continuing, 'Well, you're talking to one right now!' And he would go on to give his testimony.

One day Kenan met an old friend from university in the

street. The friend passed by without even a glimmer of recognition. Kenan ran after him.

'Hey, how are you? Don't you remember me? It's me, Kenan!'

The friend went deathly pale.

'Kenan? I was told that you'd gone to England and died.'

'Yes,' said Kenan, 'and I've come back from the dead. God has sent me with a message for you to repent!'

Jenny

While Kenan was tearing round Istanbul, Steve and Diane were quietly plotting a quite different kind of encounter. Now that he was back in Turkey, they were quite sure that this was the best time for Kenan to get married. Ever since it had become clear that the operation had been successful, they had been steadily praying in that direction. They even thought that they had found the right girl for Kenan!

When they excitedly shared their ideas with Kenan and suggested that Kenan meet up with 'their girl', he seemed rather non-commital. 'Well, maybe,' he said. 'Let's see what happens.' Jenny was still in the back of his mind, but he did not feel that he could share any thoughts about her yet; the whole idea seemed so wild anyway.

So Steve and Diane, keeping to respectable Midyat culture, invited Kenan, Mrs Araz and 'their girl' to a meal together. The girl was very nice, but Kenan knew immediately that she was not the right one for him. However, he mentioned little of his reactions to Steve and Diane, not wanting to disappoint them, and was soon back into his whirl of visits. Life was so busy during that first week back in Turkey that there was hardly time to think about girls anyway.

At the beginning of the second week Kenan was again visiting Steve and Diane's house. Steve happened to remark casually: 'By the way, did you know that Larry and Nancy have arrived back in Istanbul, and Jenny is with them?'

Jenny with them! In Istanbul! Kenan suddenly found his heart beating rather faster than usual. This was ridiculous. Why, he hardly knew the girl. He told himself to be cool and rational, but for some reason found it difficult. Perhaps his Big Father was in this as well? How extraordinary that she should arrive in Istanbul just a few days after he had arrived, especially considering the fact that he had been due there weeks before in October.

Kenan would have been even more amazed had he known how Jenny had come to be in Istanbul that week. She was actually travelling from the *m.v. Logos* (then in Kuwait) to Izmir where she intended to live. She had never planned to come to Istanbul. It was only because of a mix-up over baggage that she was there at all. In fact her arrival in Turkey had been due to many frustrating delays as well. So Kenan's delays and hers together meant that they both 'just happened' to be passing through Istanbul during the very same week . . . .

A few days later they met in a mutual friend's house. Kenan said nothing to Jenny about the growing interest he felt for her. He knew he had to be sure of his interest, otherwise he might embarrass and hurt her. Anyway, as he kept reminding himself, they hardly knew each other . . . .

The next day Kenan did something that was very typical of his gentle spirit and his desire never to hurt another brother in Christ. He knew that his old friend Shamun, who was also from Midyat and had also come to Christ in the early 1960s, had proposed to Jenny soon after he had first seen her in 1969. It was one of those precipitous proposals which are not uncommon in Turkish custom, but which Jenny, fresh from England, had found alarmingly sudden. In fact, it had been done by letter on the basis of Shamun having seen Jenny a few times in church meetings – there had been no personal meeting between them at all. Not willing to offend this Turkish brother in any way, Jenny had politely declined, and there the matter was left. But Kenan knew that Shamun had been hurt by this refusal. Now he went to him with a question: would Shamun mind if his own

interest in Jenny eventually led to marriage? The last thing
Kenan wanted was a rift in their friendship. He hated to see
friends hurt in any way. Thankfully, Shamun appeared to
be perfectly happy with the possibility and Kenan left his
house that evening greatly relieved.

Before leaving Istanbul, Kenan saw Jenny just once
more. It was on the following Sunday at the regular church
meeting. But he felt no peace to share anything with her of
his attachment. Instead he shared his thoughts with Steve
and Diane on the way home after the service and discussed
the remarkable way in which Jenny had come to Istanbul
from Kuwait so soon after he had arrived from England.
Steve and Diane were impressed. It certainly seemed an extraordinary coincidence. For his part, Kenan kept on saying: 'I'm not really sure yet. I don't want to say anything to
Jenny. I don't want to hurt her if she doesn't feel the same
interest in me.'

Finally Steve said, 'Look, I think the best thing would be
if you left this in our hands. You're leaving for Midyat tomorrow anyway and you're not going to see Jenny again for
a while. Let's pray about it and if we find an opportunity,
Diane can tell Jenny what you've told us and see her reaction. If she's not interested, the whole thing can stop there
with no bad feelings. But if she *is* interested, at least you
could start to correspond with her.'

Kenan felt peace about this and agreed. The next day he
and his mother left for Midyat.

A few days later Jenny went to visit Diane. Diane was ill
in bed and Jenny went up to talk to her. Within a few minutes Diane plunged into the story about Kenan. As Jenny
listened, she was filled with many conflicting emotions.
That almost-forgotten night in London when she had knelt
in prayer for Kenan's healing and had experienced that sudden inner conviction that she would marry him, suddenly
came swimming back into her consciousness. Yet there
were also many doubts. She had noticed that Kenan's English was still not very good and her Turkish was distinctly
weak, to say the least. At the same time Jenny was under no

illusions as to the potential problems of cross-cultural marriages. She had seen enough of them in action to know that they took extra grace and maturity to be successful.

As Diane talked, Jenny's face mirrored the many different thoughts passing through her mind. Diane had been half-expecting her to come out with a forthright 'No'. When it became clear that this was not Jenny's immediate response, Diane jumped out of bed excitedly and ran downstairs to tell Steve: 'Steve!' she shouted. 'She didn't say "No"! She didn't say "No"!' How much Steve and Diane loved Kenan! They were so longing for him to get married. But in Jenny's heart many questions remained.

Kenan is back!

Meanwhile down in Midyat Kenan was receiving such a rumbustious welcome that any thought of Jenny and marriage was quickly swept from his mind. A large crowd had gathered to welcome them and escort them triumphantly the last few hundred yards to the familiar grey-stone house in 'Little Lake' on the outskirts of the town. Clouds of dust rose in the air and little children ran up and down shouting, 'Look, see, Kenan is back! Kenan is back!' Above the shouting could be heard the exultant shrill sound of the *kileli*. There at the large wooden door of the house Mr Araz stood waiting, surrounded by Kenan's brother and sisters, all craning their necks to be the first to catch a glimpse of their mother and Kenan. Unable to contain themselves any longer, they ran forward into the crowd and within a few seconds the whole family were in each other's arms.

That evening several sheep were killed and a great feast was laid on at the Araz household. The eldest son had returned! Relatives and neighbours crowded the dining room, and visitors continued to stream into the house until late into the night. How fit Mrs Araz looked, although she now had only one kidney! And how plump Kenan looked ! The old ladies who came to visit pinched his cheeks and several tried to see if they could feel the extra kidney. For

Kenan it was a relief when the final visitors bade their
farewells – he was beginning to feel like a prize specimen in
some kind of public show!

That night he felt too tired to sleep. When all the household was quiet, he slipped out onto the balcony that over-
looked the inner courtyard. Over the little town there was
utter stillness. Above him the heavens seemed to be car-
peted with stars, so bright and so close that Kenan drew his
breath. Living in big cities like Istanbul and London, where
the glare of artificial light obscured the brightness of the
stars, he had almost forgotten the sense of awe that now returned to him as he stared up into the immensity of the
night sky. His God – his Big Father – was the very same God
who was holding each one of those stars in place! Kenan
felt very humbled as he realised afresh that the God who
held the stars in place was the same God who was interested in every detail of his life.

Through the gloom of the courtyard, the outlines of the
old stone house built for the missionaries so many years
before stood out clearly against the stars. From the slender
crescent of the moon emanated a dim light that was just
sufficient to pick out the place where the wooden door led
into the dark shadow of the cellar under the house. Yes, the
God who held the stars in place was the same God who
could give great joy to men as they were crammed into a
filthy prison waiting to be executed. In one sense, thought
Kenan, it seemed more of a miracle than holding the stars
in place for people to have joy in the midst of suffering; joy
when the story had an unhappy ending; joy even when
there was no apparent reason for the suffering.

Kenan's mind drifted back over the past year. How
amazing that God had also given him great joy, even when
he had faced almost certain death. He remembered the
great surge of joy that had come to him just before being
wheeled into the operating theatre. Tonight he had seen
such joy written on people's faces as the result of his
triumphant return to Midyat. But what would have
happened if this story had not had a happy ending? What

would have happened if they had not all ended up in each other's arms? What then?

Thoughtfully, Kenan turned and headed back to bed.

The preacher with three kidneys

During the following weeks Kenan lost no opportunity in using the publicity surrounding his transplant to share the gospel. He suddenly found himself speaking from church pulpits that, in the normal course of events, would never have been open to him. In Protestant, Orthodox and Catholic Assyrian churches, he was able to speak directly but simply of God's power to answer prayer and to give new life to diseased bodies and broken spirits. People would ask others, 'Have you ever heard a preacher who has three kidneys?' Of course they had not, so the churches would fill up with a crowd of curious listeners.

Sympathetic and gentle when witnessing to his many Muslim friends, Kenan was often very blunt when speaking to nominal Christians from his own community. So many believed that they could somehow be Christians by virtue of birth into an Assyrian family. Even worse, in Kenan's eyes, were the attitudes of pride and superiority toward their Muslim neighbours, simply because they believed that they had a 'superior religion'. Kenan knew from his own experience that, morally, there was little difference between a nominal Muslim and a nominal Christian. In God's eyes, both were in the same boat anyway – faced with a yawning chasm that separated them from a holy God, which could only be crossed by means of a personal, saving knowledge of Christ. No Christian had the slightest grounds for boasting or for feeling superior. One Christian talking to another person about his faith was just like one beggar telling another beggar where to find bread.

After travelling and speaking in the Midyat and Mardin areas, Kenan moved on to visit his many relatives in northern Syria. There also he found the Assyrian churches open to him. From Syria he went on to Lebanon, and the pattern was again repeated. The community 'network' in these countries soon passed him on to the next friend or contact and Kenan became known throughout as 'the man with three kidneys'.

Often he would have to pinch himself to make sure that it was not all a dream. Only a year ago he had lain dying in hospital. Now here he was preaching to hundreds of people all over the Middle East. Kenan knew that even if he had spent years in England obtaining the best theological degrees he would still have had problems in being able to speak in some of these churches. Yet with no paper qualifications at all, but with an extra kidney on board, all doors were seemingly open to him!

The long weeks of travel finally over, Kenan went back to Midyat for a while. Then came the time to return to London for his next check-up. At St Mary's Hospital all the reports were good. The extra kidney seemed to be in excellent condition. The doctors gave their final verdict that Kenan could return and settle in Turkey. There was of course always the possibility that his body would reject the new kidney at any time, so Kenan would have to return to London every three to four months for a check-up. In addition, he would need to send a blood sample to St Mary's every month as an extra precaution.

While Kenan was enjoying his final months in England, Jenny was settling down to regular Turkish studies in Izmir. Winter had come and gone. On the central Anatolian plateau it had been one of the coldest winters for years. Many had died from the cold, and hungry wolves had been seen on the outskirts of even the larger cities. But in Izmir the winter had passed almost unnoticed and the balmy days of spring were already with them. Sometimes Jenny's thoughts would turn to Kenan, but her emotions remained confused. How could two people from such different backgrounds have a successful marriage?

One day a letter arrived from Kenan in London. Would Jenny like to correspond? Once again Jenny was full of doubts. Where would it all lead? She set aside regular times each week for prayer and fasting about the situation, and it was during these times that God gave her real peace to continue with the relationship. So they started to write to each other. From the beginning, the correspondence was conducted in Turkish.

Finally, in May 1972 Kenan returned to settle in Istanbul. It was decided that Jenny should come up from Izmir to stay with Steve and Diane so that she and Kenan would have opportunities to meet in a respectable way without offending cultural sensibilities.

From the beginning they were amazed at how quickly they were able to get to know each other. Though so different in background, it seemed that God had been preparing the one for the other. During those blissfully happy days of late May and early June they wandered the parks of Istanbul, which were resplendent in their crop of early summer blooms, sipping tea together on little quayside tea-houses overlooking the bustling waterway of the Golden Horn. They also spent time visiting many friends and relatives in Istanbul so that Jenny could fully appreciate what it would mean to marry into the Araz family. Jenny understood enough of Turkish culture to know that if she married Kenan she would not be marrying just an individual, but would be becoming part of an extended family, a family that would expect her to play a certain role and fulfill certain responsibilities.

Steve and Diane stayed discreetly in the background, quietly delighted as they watched Kenan and Jenny fall in love. There was no need to ask Jenny how things were going when she returned home in the evenings; her slightly flushed cheeks and willing smile told their own story.

Suddenly, in the middle of June, the spell was broken. Kenan had just sent a blood sample to St Mary's. Two days later an urgent telegram arrived from London that quickly blew to bits his euphoria. It read:

'BLOOD TESTS SHOW HIGH LEVEL OF POISON STOP INCREASE YOUR DRUGS FORTY PER CENT STOP PLEASE COME TO ENGLAND ON NEXT PLANE STOP

Kenan was shattered. He could not believe it. Surely there must be some mistake. He felt as fit as he ever had. Besides, being in love made him feel even fitter. Jenny, too, felt very disturbed. Was she going to lose Kenan so soon when God just seemed to be leading them together so wonderfully?

Kenan and Jenny prayed together. Then, very reluctantly, he obeyed the doctors' orders, borrowing some money so that he could make the expensive flight to London. It was a Saturday. When he reached Heathrow Airport, Kenan rang through to the hospital:

'This is Kenan. I've arrived and I thought I'd call at the hospital sometime.'

The nurse on the other end of the line sounded deadly serious: 'Kenan, don't talk too much. You're desperately ill. Get in a taxi and come immediately.'

When Kenan arrived at the hospital, nurses hurried up to him with serious faces. 'Don't talk. You're very ill. Quickly, undress, into bed . . . .'

Kenan protested in vain: 'I feel very well, really. It must be a mistake . . . .'

But he was soon bundled into bed and receiving painful spinal injections before being put onto special machines and drips.

Kenan thoughtfully surveyed the paraphenalia surrounding him. It was all very hard to believe. It was almost as if he was back at the beginning again. Yet in spite of everything the doctors said, he still had the deep conviction that it must be a mistake, and told them so as they made their various examinations. They smiled weakly and said:

'We'll tell you on Monday when we get the final results.'

From his bed, Kenan phoned various close friends in London. One of them, Phil, came to see him on Sunday.

'Phil,' he said, 'look, I'm perfectly all right. The doctors must have made a mistake.'

Phil shook his head solemnly. 'Don't get excited, brother; you're very ill. Let's pray about it.'

Kenan counted the hours and minutes up to seven o'clock on Monday evening when the results would be ready. He hated to be back in a hospital bed with drips and machines around him. It brought back so many memories, memories that he would rather forget.

Promptly at seven on Monday evening the door burst open and the doctor came running into his room with a sheet of paper in his hand.

'Kenan!' he exclaimed. 'You're all right! There's been a terrible mistake! You're perfectly well. Somehow your blood sample must have got mixed up with someone else's!'

Kenan gave a great big smile and started pulling the drip out of his arm before a nurse hurriedly stopped him!

'*Hamd olsun! Hamd olsun!* See, it's my Big Father!'

Within a few days he was back in Istanbul. After some correspondence, the hospital admitted their fault in mixing the blood samples and calling Kenan to London – an extremely rare error in a very efficiently run hospital. In fact they were so apologetic that they offered to cover all Kenan's expenses, including the return air fare to London. Kenan saw it all as just one more example of God's love and concern for him. It was good to feel so secure in the plan of a God who knew best . . . .

Marriage

In July, Kenan and Jenny became officially engaged. Jenny's family came to Istanbul from England to share the joy of the engagement. Kenan was overjoyed at their positive attitude towards him. Ever since his experience with Anda he had been afraid that parental pressure might make marriage to Jenny impossible. But from the outset, Jenny's family had backed her up completely in her decision. This meant a lot to both of them, and when her family finally met Kenan in July, they loved him – they loved him for his big smile, his warm generous heart and his obvious deep regard and affection for Jenny.

Kenan and Jenny decided to get married in Jenny's church back in England. The date was set for 30 September, but first there was the long bureaucratic process preparing for the legal side of the marriage in Turkey. This was doubly complicated by the fact that Jenny was a foreigner. It involved a short ceremony in the Turkish equivalent of a registry office, the only place where weddings in Turkey can be legally carried out. Kenan and Jenny had already decided that they would not view this as their 'real' wedding – that would be the church service in England. Nevertheless they had to go through with it so that they could obtain the legal rights of a married couple in Turkey.

During the coming months Kenan spent many frustrating hours going from one office to another trying to get the vital marriage papers processed. At the same time he had another worry on his mind. How could he cope financially with setting up home and supporting a wife, and at the same time making the regular trips to London for medical check-ups? Kenan had already calculated that it would cost him around 15,000 to 18,000 Turkish lira per year just to fly to London and back, in those days a very large sum. How could he possibly find that kind of money? God had provided wonderfully for the cost of the operation, but he could not expect to live off other people's generosity forever. Kenan was only too aware of the many New Testament passages that exhorted the believers to work and 'be dependent on nobody'.

For a start Kenan decided to complete the civil engineering exams so that he could obtain his degree, at the same time using the months which led up to the exams to turn his hands to various jobs that seemed to hold out the promise of quick money. One project was to export Turkish bric-à-brac, but this provided little income. Other projects were even less profitable.

How could they plan to get married in England when

Kenan could not even make enough money for the air fare? He would often pray over the situation with Jenny.

One day in August, while Kenan was praying, he suddenly had an idea. It was a wild idea, but Kenan knew from previous experience that his wild ideas sometimes had an uncanny way of working out. His idea was this: perhaps if he went to the Turkish Airlines company, they would give him a reduced fare or even a free ticket to London! After all, a Turk with three kidneys did not travel on a *THY* plane every day, so perhaps it would be a good piece of promotion for them. Smiling to himself at the absurdity of his mission, Kenan set off the next morning to the Turkish Airlines office near Taksim Square. He introduced himself to the girl at reception and explained what he wanted. She looked at him in total amazement.

'I'm sorry, sir,' she said, 'but I don't think we can help you.' Then, so as not to hurt his feelings, she added, 'But why not write out an official request and bring it back here tomorrow.'

So Kenan went away and composed his request. He explained everything about his operation and the necessity to go regularly to London for check-ups. Then, at the bottom of the letter, as a wild afterthought, Kenan added a postscript: 'By the way, I'm getting married soon. Is it possible to give me a ticket for my wife as well?'

The next day Kenan returned to the office and presented his written request. The receptionist read it and began to laugh.

'This is utterly impossible,' she said. 'They'll never give you this. They don't even know you! I'm sorry, but we can't help you.'

'I know,' said Kenan, 'it certainly does seem impossible, but just pass it on to your boss anyway. At least let him make the final decision.'

So, under protest, the girl took the request and passed it through the right channels. Kenan took his leave and, in the frantic activities of the next few days, virtually forgot about the whole idea. The initial reaction had been so negative anyway.

Three weeks later Kenan and Jenny were at his uncle's house. It was about noontime when Kenan's young cousin came running up the stairs. 'There are two strange men downstairs asking for you. They want to speak with you. Come quickly!'

Kenan and Jenny looked at each other. The same thought was passing through both their minds. Probably it was the police. Kenan had already been involved in various literature projects since returning to Turkey. There was always the possibility that he would be followed and picked up for questioning.

Jenny went into a back room to pray while Kenan went downstairs to greet the two men.

'Are you Kenan Araz?' they asked.

'Yes,' said Kenan. 'Can I help you?'

'Well, we're from Turkish Airlines and we're here to tell you that the company will be happy to give both you and your wife a free ticket to go to London for your check-up whenever you want. The only thing we need to know is, what date do you want to go next?'

Kenan nearly fell off his chair. Then he jumped up with a great smile and, shaking their hands again, started to tell them all about his Big Father and how he had prayed for those tickets!

To Kenan and Jenny it was just another sign that God was in control of their lives down to the finest detail. The God who cared about the big life and death things like kidneys and operations was also the same God who was involved in every minutia of their lives. 'Seek *first* the kingdom of God . . . and all these *other* things . . . .'

Mid-September came and still the vital marriage documents had not been processed. Kenan and Jenny were praying hard. How could they face Jenny's family if they were forced to postpone the wedding date? Jenny cringed inwardly at the thought. The invitations had gone out and all had been made ready. It was only after a good Turkish friend had gone to the relevant ministry in Ankara on their behalf that it was discovered that the crucial document had been blown into a corner by a puff of wind and forgotten!

At last the precious premission was brought back to Istanbul; it was Tuesday, 19 September. All Kenan and Jenny had to do now was book an official wedding in the registry office and they would then be free to travel to England for the church wedding.

Early next morning Kenan prepared to set off for the local registry office. Because he lived in a certain area of Istanbul, it was the only place where he and Jenny could be married.

'I think you should come with me,' Kenan said to Jenny. 'I'd like you to be with me. You never know what might happen.'

They reached the registry office at ten o'clock. The clerk looked through his books. 'Well, we have a lot of weddings coming up. I think I could put you down for a fortnight's time.' A fortnight's time! Oh, no – the wedding in England was now only ten days away. Besides this, Kenan needed to go very soon to London to have a check-up. Four months had already gone by since he had returned to settle in Turkey, which meant that his next check-up was long overdue.

Kenan explained all this to the clerk. 'Well, all right,' he finally said. 'Maybe I can fit you in during the lunch break. Come back today at twelve o'clock with two witnesses.' Twelve o'clock! It was now ten-thirty, so there was no time to lose. Jenny raced home to get changed while Kenan hurried off in search of suitable witnesses. First he went to his uncle's shop, which was not far away, and his uncle promised to come. From there he went to his cousin's business, but his cousin was out, and another cousin who lived down the road was out too. By now time was very short. Kenan leaped into a taxi and by eleven-thirty had arrived at the home of Steve and Diane. Diane was in hospital after the birth of their fourth child, Ruth, so Steve was at home looking after the children. Kenan burst into the house excitedly: 'Steve, you've got to come with me. I'm getting married in half an hour. You've got to be my witness'‡

Even the phlegmatic Steve was a little taken aback but, nothing daunted, left the children with a neighbour and jumped into the taxi with Kenan.

At twelve o'clock sharp Kenan arrived back at the registry office. His uncle was already there, along with his aunt, his sister Habibe, and Jenny. They were ushered into the large and impressive wedding hall – the largest in Istanbul – which normally would be packed with hundreds of guests. Kenan, Jenny and the two breathless witnesses climbed up onto the platform and sat down at a large table. A sea of empty chairs stretched away into the distance. In the middle of this 'wasteland' sat Kenan's aunt with Habibe. Steve had great difficulty in not laughing as the pompous-looking registrar in black robes climbed ponderously onto the platform, solemnly took the microphone and began his speech to the huge empty hall:

'We are *all* gathered here to witness . . . .'

The whole event was like a comedy act and Kenan and Jenny felt no more married when they re-emerged into the bright sunshine outside than when they had gone in; but in their hands was the precious wedding certificate. Now, officially man and wife, they were eligible for the free *THY* air tickets. Kenan hurried off to the airline office to make the arrangements. On Saturday they flew to London with just a week left to help in the preparations for the big day. On Monday Kenan went to St Mary's for his check-up and was declared fit and healthy. The new kidney was working perfectly.

There was a small detail about their marriage that still seemed totally unclear. Jenny had first raised the subject some weeks earlier while they were still in Istanbul:

'Er, Kenan,' she had started, 'we have this custom in England. When we get married . . . we usually go for a week's honeymoon . . . but, we don't have anywhere to go, do we . . . ?'

It was true. They had nowhere to go. They had just

enough money for daily necessities, that was all. Kenan's reply was characteristic: 'Don't worry, my love, let's pray about it. My Big Father knows what we need. What we must be sure about is that we're living in day-by-day obedience to him.' So they had prayed, and left their need happily with God. Now and again Jenny had daydreamed wistfully of the two of them setting out to go on their honeymoon at some luxury hotel, but each time she had managed in the end, after some struggle, to leave the matter once again with God.

Now there were just a few days to go before the wedding and still they had no idea what they were going to do afterwards. Relatives were dropping hints to try and find out where they were going, but fortunately the veil of secrecy traditionally surrounding such events allowed Kenan and Jenny to smile quietly, as if their dream honeymoon plans were far too private to reveal.

When they finally arrived at Jenny's home, a large pile of letters was waiting for them, mostly replies from friends who were coming to the wedding. They started opening and reading them. Suddenly Kenan jumped up, a broad grin spread across his face and he started dancing round the room. *'Hamd olsun* . . . See how good my Big Father is!'

The letter in his hand was from some close friends of Jenny: 'We are looking forward to seeing you at your wedding . . . . And as a wedding present we have booked a week's holiday for you at a hotel in the country, full board, everything included, all paid for . . . .'

Kenan gave Jenny a big hug: 'You see, my Big Father hasn't forgotten us!'

The wedding on Saturday, 30 September, 1972, was a very happy time. The sun shone, the church was packed, and as Kenan and Jenny stood together at the front of the church, they felt as if the great volume of praise being offered up behind them was summing up all the miracles, both big and small, that God had accomplished to bring them together that day.

After Kenan had promised to love Jenny in sickness and

in health and had completed the normal wedding vows, he suddenly turned to her with a tender smile and spontaneously came out with something extra:

'And I promise to tell her every day about my Big Father!'

That is exactly what Kenan did. Sometimes in later years, if he was feeling at all depressed and the situation seemed too hard to bear, Jenny would gently remind him: 'Come on, you promised to tell me every day about your Big Father!' Then Kenan would start to remember all the good things that had happened to him and soon his heart would be praising again.

At the wedding reception Kenan rose to his feet to make his speech, smiling especially at different faces in the crowd as he recognised each of them.

'During the last few years,' Kenan began, 'God has given me many new things. Ten years ago my Big Father gave me a *new heart*, to know him personally and to live for him. Then again, one and a half years ago, my Big Father gave me a *new kidney* to live for him for a short time longer. And now my big Father has given me a *new wife!*'

Kenan was so happy with his Big Father, and it seemed also in the weeks and months that followed that his Big Father was happy with him.

10
Turning Point

As Kenan and Jenny returned to Turkey after their honey-moon, so many different aspects of their lives seemed to fall into place. They had nowhere to live in Istanbul, but a friend provided a flat for a nominal rent. Having qualified as a civil engineer, Kenan was able to obtain a number of jobs that provided money for their daily needs. Gradually they settled down into a new pattern of life. For the first time in years Kenan felt that he was 'normal' – he could eat and work and join in the life of the local church. As he remarked to a friend at the time:

'I thank the Lord in the morning when I'm shaving as I look in the mirror to see that my face isn't yellow anymore, and when I eat an egg at breakfast and when I drink a glass of water.'

Just as peace can only really be appreciated after a time of war, so the privilege of good health can only really be understood after a time of prolonged illness. For Kenan all the simple events of daily life became infused with new meaning and value. He had been close to death so many times that the very act of living became filled with a new quality of joy.

There was nothing that Kenan and Jenny enjoyed more than welcoming visitors into their home. From the moment their little flat was established, a steady stream of people began to come. Many were Kenan's old Muslim friends. Many others were from the Assyrian, Armenian and Greek communities in the city. Since Jenny was British the house also became a 'dropping-in place' for relatives and friends from abroad.

Kenan always felt most relaxed at home. In fact he enjoyed times of informal fellowship with small groups of

Christian friends at home far more than fellowship at the
church meetings. The local church, which had started with
Kenan and the others in the 1960s, had indeed grown considerably. Many, mainly from nominal Christian
backgrounds, had continued to come to Christ. A hundred
or more were now coming to the meetings.

Many of the believers in the church in Istanbul had a real
evangelistic zeal. They were often rather blunt and over-di-
rect in their approach to Muslims; nevertheless they would
go out on the main streets of Istanbul openly distributing
Bibles and other Christian literature. Kenan rejoiced in this
outreach, in seeing people actively going out with the gospel. He also rejoiced in the greater spirit of freedom that
was beginning to come into the meetings. For a time even
cymbals, tambourines and other instruments made an appearance during worship and many new hymns were introduced. As long as the emphasis was on a spirit of joyful
worship the church stayed together. But somehow the
main leadership of the church was never really able to
shake off the heavy religious legacy of the Mardin monasteries. Doctrinal squabbles of Byzantine intricacy would
frequently disrupt church life.

Kenan could not feel completely at home in the church
because he sensed no genuine acceptance. No church can
flourish without mutual acceptance of its members. As
Kenan sat at the Lord's Table, it was difficult to forget that,
incredible though it might seem, there were others sitting
there who still felt that his operation had demonstrated
lack of faith, that the doctors who had cared for him in London with such concern and patience were little more than
'butchers', and that he should have 'trusted God alone' for
his healing. Kenan had forgiven his brothers from the bottom of his heart. Yet forgiveness was one thing – being able
to forget was another.

In the eyes of some, Kenan had never lost the label of
being *hafif*. He did not wallow, as did some, in an introspective and morbid fascination with his own sinfulness and
corruption. Kenan was too full of Jesus to worry too much

about that. In the meetings he would always choose cheerful hymns, the praising hymns, but these would often be lost in a plethora of long and doleful hymns, full of self-recrimination on the evils of the flesh and the hardness and narrowness of the true way. It was not that the theology of the other hymns was untrue – it was more a question of balance. With a leadership unknowingly committed to various neo-Platonic views about the body, inherited from their Orthodox church backgrounds, the fellowship was wide open to all kinds of tangents and tangled doctrinal emphases.

For a time almost the whole church became taken up with the teachings of Watchman Nee. There is, of course, much useful teaching in the writings of Watchman Nee, but pure undiluted Watchman Nee, week after week, month after month, taken in large doses and without the balancing effect that reading other Christian authors can bring, led, as might be expected, to the embroiling of believers in complex theological discussions. Some of these dissertations made the (probably apocryphal) story of Byzantine worthies of the Constantinople of an earlier age discussing how many angels could dance on a pin-head, look quite mild by comparison. One of the main debates centred around the exact relationship between the body, soul and spirit, and as to what exactly the Holy Spirit was doing in each particular sphere of the believer's life. Forgetting that the Bible itself shows a singular lack of interest in defining such things, indeed not infrequently using the terms 'soul' and 'spirit' almost interchangeably, and forgetting the many examples of Christians who try to tie up into tidy theological boxes matters which God never intended so to be tied, the believers of the Istanbul fellowship proceeded to batter one another with verses on this subject, finding support for their various positions in the more esoteric writings of Nee.

After one of these sterile discussions, Kenan emerged from the dark recesses of the meeting place into the bright sunshine outside, and uttered a phrase that was overheard by several and thereafter must surely have contributed to

his reputation for being *hafif*. Although no doubt losing
something in translation, it is nevertheless worth explaining the phrase as it expresses something of his attitude to
such matters. The word 'soul' in Turkish is *jan*, and *patla* is
the root of the verb 'to explode'. *Patlajan* is the word for
aubergine, a vegetable that plays a major role in Turkish
cooking. Kenan came out of church that morning exclaim-
ing: '*Jan, jan, patlajan!*'

This could be loosely translated, 'My soul, my soul,
explode my soul!' or, alternatively, 'My soul, my soul, aubergine!'

While not profound as a theological comment on the de-
bate in question, the phrase nevertheless expressed the
feelings of more than one of those present.

To the end of his days Kenan had a simple, direct faith in
God. It was not simple in the sense of being simplistic – he
was too intelligent for that – but it was the kind of faith that
had a distaste for tortuous arguments and theoretical discussions. For example, Kenan believed that what happened in the daily life of the Christian's home was of far
more importance than the eloquence with which that
Christian could pray or preach in church. This, unfortunately, was a point not always heeded by the more 'super-
spiritual' members of the church.

There were numerous attempts to appoint recognised elders in the growing fellowship, but for one reason or
another these attempts invariably foundered. Kenan was
himself appointed an elder at one stage, but never felt very
happy about it. He believed that his gifts, though clearly
pastoral, were better used in a quieter, more personal way,
aside from the noisy discussions and heated recrimina-
tions that by now had unfortunately become associated
with the appointment of elders.

Another aspect of church life that Kenan found disap-
pointing was the fact that there was still no place where he
could freely take those of his Muslim friends who were
showing an interest in the gospel. The church consisted almost entirely of people from a nominal Christian

background. Because of his own upbringing Kenan knew how difficult it was for a Muslim Turk, even one who had professed Christ, to feel relaxed and accepted in that atmosphere.

One problem was the legalism. There were educated Turks who were seriously seeking God, but who were sick of the lists of rules they found in Islam. Yet even with those who professed Christ, Kenan hesitated from trying to draw them into the fellowship, feeling that he would only be transferring them from one form of legalism to another.

Another problem, common to many churches in the Middle East, was that Muslim converts would either feel a certain coldness and suspicion towards them arising from the centuries of separation between the Christian and Muslim communities or, the opposite side of the same coin, the church would make a great fuss of the convert, hailing him with great publicity as 'a transfer from the Muslim side to the Christian side', until the poor man had either been destroyed spiritually by pride or physically by the wrath of his relatives as they reacted to the publicity. The one thing the Muslim convert was longing for – to be accepted in a friendly way in the church as a normal human being, saved by grace like anyone else – was sadly lacking.

So Kenan and Jenny soon found that while much of their fellowship was centred around the church, most of their outreach to their Muslim friends was on a quite different level. Although Christian books, pamphlets, radio and correspondence course work were all crucial for the sowing of the seed of the kingdom, Kenan and Jenny saw clearly that it was only through spending hour after hour with their Muslim friends in personal witness that the breakthroughs were going to come and a church, still in the future, was going to be born in which the ninety-nine percent majority of Turks in the country would themselves constitute the largest group.

Kenan had a simple but direct way of sharing his faith with Muslims. He rarely became involved in discussions about the Qur'an and Mohammed. As he was fond of telling his guests, that was *their* area of expertise, not his. But Kenan pointed much to Jesus. He talked of his power to heal and to forgive, of his majesty, of his love for the sinner. As Jesus was lifted up as the only Saviour of the world, so people began to be drawn to him. Not many were converted then as a direct result of the witness of Kenan and Jenny, but many heard and understood the gospel clearly for the first time and, years later, could still remember the powerful impact that the couple's friendship had made on their lives.

I'm a Turk!

Kenan's love for Turkey and the Turks made it easy and natural for him to share the gospel with Turks. He was accepted as one of them, and felt very strongly about his own Turkishness. Indeed, it was one of the few subjects about which he could be rather fierce.

Sometimes Jenny would start explaining to a foreign friend that Kenan was from Midyat, and that he was an Assyrian, but Kenan would become quite angry. 'No! I'm a Turk!' he would burst out. He hated anything that would break that identity and was appalled by the lengths to which Assyrians, emigrating as workers to Europe, would go in espousing their Assyrian nationalistic causes.

In 1974 Kenan attended the World Congress of Evangelism in Lausanne as part of the group of official Turkish delegates, half of whom in fact were from nominal Christian backgrounds. On the first day of the Congress all the delegates were asked to wear badges showing their names and which country they were representing. One of the members of the delegation wrote on his badge his name and 'Armenian'. It took a lot to get Kenan angry. On this occasion he was really roused. 'You're not from Armenia; you're from Turkey! You – are – Turkish!' he yelled. It was just as well so many people were in the vicinity, otherwise the offending badge might have been ripped off there and then!

Soon after Kenan and Jenny came back to live in Istanbul, the law was changed in England, to give foreign husbands married to English women the right to settle permanently in England. Kenan's Turkish friends could not understand why they continued to live in Turkey. Kenan and Jenny had every reason to settle in England. Life there was so much easier: there were so many goods in the shops, the hospital was much closer for emergencies, etc . . . . So the reasons would be piled up, all good and logical, but so far from that solemn vow that remained in the depths of Kenan's heart that, as the Lord had given his life back, so he would give the remaining years of his life one hundred per cent to God's work in Turkey.

Although their Turkish friends could not really understand why Kenan and Jenny stayed in Turkey, they certainly respected them for it. Kenan saw very clearly what others have not always seen, that the key to the Turkish heart lies not in trying to mimic the religious habits and customs of Turks – of little relevance anyway as Islam continues to lose its religious grip upon the urbanised masses – but in identifying with Turkish nationalism, that strong and continuing flow in which the figure of Kemal Ataturk still plays a central role and in which Islam is more of a symbol of national solidarity than a religion actually to be practised.

Kenan would often share with Christian friends another reason why he felt happier in Turkey:

'In England,' he would say, 'it's easy to live as a Christian; things run so smoothly. But here in Turkey there are so many difficulties – lies, bribes, endless bureaucracy, political revolution and struggles. God uses all of these to encourage us to live closer to him, so that day by day we have to become more dependent on his strength. Why,' Kenan would finish, 'living here is like a crash course in sanctification. What a privilege!'

It was perhaps the whole area of work and money that Kenan found the greatest challenge of all. Unlike some in the Istanbul church at that time, Kenan did not try to make

an artificial separation between secular work and the
Lord's work. They were all part of *one* world and *one*
integrated life that God was making new every day by the
power of his Holy Spirit. There was no way that one could
remain faithful to the Bible while claiming that to be
supported by Christians in 'full-time work' was in some
sense more spiritual or sacrificial than the person earning
his daily living in a regular job. Kenan saw clearly that the
Bible taught the validity of *both* means of support and that
Paul – and others like him – in fact experienced both during
their lives, sometimes being supported by local churches
and sometimes working hard at their chosen professions.

Kenan's first vision when he had returned to Turkey after
the operation had been to serve God in some full-time
capacity. He felt that this would be the best way in which he
could fulfill his solemn vow. So he had applied to work with
the Bible Society in Scripture distribution, but was turned
down, since the Turkish Bible Society of that time felt that
he would be a little too 'evangelical' for them. Undaunted,
Kenan became the representative of Living Bibles
International (LBI) in Turkey, which were then sponsoring
a new translation of the New Testament into modern,
contemporary and readable Turkish, the kind of Turkish
that people read every day in their newspapers. Kenan
soon became very convinced about this project, mainly
because, from the outset, the central aim of the project was
not to produce a more literal translation (though this would
have been acceptable to all the churches) but, rather, of
producing something that would be both faithful to the
original text and at the same time intelligible for all the
Turkish people.

Soon Kenan was opening an office and employing a
helper for the translation work. Much of the work involved
liaison with the translator, himself a convert from Islam,
and then testing the newly-translated materials to see how
they were received by a randomly-selected group of
readers.

For this job with LBI Kenan received a regular salary. At

first he saw this as God's provision, especially as it allowed him to carry on with various other projects. But as time went by he began to have increasing doubts about the wisdom of receiving money from a foreign Christian organisation. These doubts were increased by an incident that occurred when Kenan was returning to Istanbul through Germany after one of his periodic check-ups. Since his old friend Dale was then living in Austria, Kenan decided to drop by and see him. Dale, who never lost an opportunity to share the gospel with Turks, took Kenan to a nearby village to meet a group of immigrant Turkish workers who were interested in the gospel.

As Kenan stood up before this group to tell them of what God had done in his life, the men were rather hostile, but at the end one of the friendlier workers called him aside to pose a question: 'Tell me,' he said, 'how much did your American friend pay you to come and say these things to us? If I say I'm a Christian, will he pay me too?' Kenan was aghast. So that was why this man was so friendly! It was clear that he had not really heard the gospel at all; the expectation of easy money had become a barrier to the good news.

As Kenan returned to Istanbul the following day, he pondered deeply on the whole question of receiving foreign money as a salary. How easily could his Turkish Muslim friends say that he had become a Christian so as to make money! Most of them knew that he had an office and a secretary. At the same time it would just underline to them what they believed already – Christianity was a western imperialistic religion, channelling money wherever necessary to undermine the unity and cohesion of the Turkish people. And how could the growing Turkish Church learn responsibility in giving, so long as foreign money was pouring in from outside? Kenan knew of examples from so many different countries where foreign money flowing into the local churches had caused power struggles, disunity and many heartaches.

By the time Kenan arrived in Istanbul, his mind was already made up. For the sake of his testimony, for the sake of his Muslim friends, for the sake of the Turkish Church, he would ask LBI not to send any more salary. He sat down and carefully wrote out a politely-worded letter: yes, he would still like to claim expenses for the office and secretary, but he would rather they sent no more money for his own salary.

So Kenan went back to civil engineering, for half of each day at least, and for the rest of his life simultaneously juggled his LBI work and various engineering projects. In this way he captured the real spirit of 'tent-making' – the ability to move between a so-called secular job and Christian work, and witness so smoothly that all could be seen as part and parcel of the same integrated lifestyle.

Turning point

Throughout these years, Kenan faithfully took his ten white pills every day, drugs carefully worked out by St Mary's to prevent the rejection of his new kidney. The act of taking the pills itself was a reminder of the miracle organ filtering his blood inside him each day.

During one of his routine check-ups at St Mary's, Kenan said to one of the junior doctors: 'What does the result look like?' Teasingly, the junior doctor pulled a straight face and said solemnly: 'I think you'll die soon.' Kenan's face burst into its great smile and he cried: '*Hamd olsun!*' as he started dancing round the room. The nurse started to laugh. 'You can't frighten him!' she said.

In fact it was at the end of this test that Kenan was declared so well that from then on he would need to come to London only every five to six months. Also it would no longer be necessary to send the monthly blood samples. As a bonus it seemed that his two wasted and diseased kidneys were beginning to regain some life and strength and were beginning to function slightly. So Kenan used to tease his mother: 'Pretty soon I'll be giving your kidney back to you!'

Jenny almost came to believe it. Kenan looked so normal and he could now work almost as long a day as a person who had his own healthy kidneys. Jenny knew that Kenan often pushed himself much too hard, especially when he was organising several projects at the same time. Few people realised what a dynamo of energy there was under that cheerful face and phlegmatic exterior.

It was a good time to live and work in Turkey. The army intervention of 1970 already seemed a long time in the past, and the army had handed back power to the civilian government. Bulent Ecevit was in the ascendancy and various reforms led to a period of increased freedom. With the Turkish invasion of Cyprus in 1974, the country seemed more united than it had been for years. There were widely held hopes that a moderately left-of-centre government under the newly-victorious and popular Ecevit could continue for many years, so ensuring certain basic freedoms. Christians were particularly optimistic that Ecevit would be more effective as prime minister in applying constitutional principles of religious freedom.

In the event none of these dreams came true. Following the Cyprus invasion the bookshops were full of hastily-written books about Ecevit, some portraying him as 'the third man', to succeed Kemal Ataturk and Ismet Inönü as the next great Turkish leader in line. But when Ecevit, riding on this new wave of popularity, went to the polls in a snap election attempting to shake off his right-wing Muslim Salvation Party coalition partner, the results were a bitter disappointment for him, and opened the way to the political return of Suleyman Demirel, the prime minister who had been forcibly removed by the army in 1970 and whom the Generals had clearly not wished to be seen holding the reins of power again.

For Turkey the year 1975 was a turning point. It was the beginning of five years of weak coalition governments in which Ecevit and Demirel bounced the post of prime minister backwards and forwards like a tennis ball. A crippling yearly bill from the army in Cyprus and spiraling world oil prices pushed Turkey into an economic abyss with enormous foreign debts and triple-figure inflation. Weak governments and economic collapse led to political violence that was to assume civil war proportions before the army would finally step in again in September 1980.

Curiously, for Kenan and Jenny too, 1975 was a turning point. The previous year had gone so well. Kenan's business had finally become established. The translation and checking work took a big step forward with the completion of John's Gospel in the new Living Version. Financially things were much easier. Kenan and Jenny were so happy together as they reached out to touch Turks with the gospel.

But the early months of 1975 were disturbingly different. First, in February, Kenan slipped on the stairs while carrying a suitcase and dislocated his arm. In the past he had dislocated the same arm several times. Somehow this time the whole experience became a nightmare. The accident happened during a freak snowstorm one Sunday morning. When Kenan and Jenny finally struggled to the hospital, there were only junior doctors on duty. The senior doctor arrived more than an hour later, having fought his way through the blizzard, but by this time muscular spasms had set in and Kenan's arm was extremely painful. Completely against his wishes, the doctor put the arm back into place under anaesthetic. (Due to his kidney transplant, the doctors at St Mary's had warned Kenan that they should be consulted about any medical decision, however small, including anaesthesia.)

During the weeks that followed, Kenan struggled along the icy streets with his arm in a sling. It was one of those lingering, grey, slushy Istanbul winters, when the mists blew in from the Marmara Sea in great swirling clouds and the fog-horns from the ferries and ships on the Bosphorous echoed around cobbled streets that were sometimes encased in a blanket of snow, but more usually oozing with the well-trodden mud left by thousands of commuting pedestrians.

Kenan's mood reflected the weather. During these months he had many frustrations with his job. Several openings appeared for building projects, only to fall through at the crucial point. Kenan was continually off-colour, not his normal cheerful self. He and Jenny tried to slow down their active way of life. They rested more in the evenings and at weekends instead of carrying on their heavy programme of visiting. But nothing seemed to help. They prayed much together, but still Kenan remained physically drained and uncharacteristically irritable. Serveral of Kenan's close friends were surprised to find that his normal flow of banter and repartee had been stopped as if in mid-flow.

For Jenny it was all very puzzling. Yet she and Kenan had weathered so many storms together that she was sure God would pull them through this one as well. She still had a deep inner conviction that God would not allow Kenan to die – after all, he had done so many miracles to bring them this far. Surely Kenan's Big Father would step in and pull him out of this spiral of depression and physical exhaustion!

Then in April, after a ten-day period of frantic activity connected with his engineering job, Kenan came home with a high temperature. Despite many visits to the doctor and numerous medications his fever remained obstinately above 41°C. Ironically it was just when he was at his lowest ebb, when Kenan desperately needed the assurance of God's love for him, that there came a visit from a group of Job's comforters. It soon emerged that they had not come to visit Kenan because he was ill, but because they wanted his professional advice on a new building project in which they were involved. Perhaps not realising the seriousness of his illness, they kept Kenan talking endlessly about the ins and outs of this project before finally coming round to the old well-worn theme. How could Kenan still be ill? Did he not think that his condition was due to some sin? Surely the way to find healing was to repent and seek God's forgiveness?

Before the astonished eyes of Jenny, and of Steve and Diane who happened to be visiting them at the same time, Kenan did not protest but obediently crawled out of bed and fell weakly to his knees. Burying his flushed face in his hands, he prayed out loud amidst the sudden hush that had fallen over them: 'Oh God, if my illness is due to any sin or hidden fault, please forgive me. My Big Father, I want to be pure, I want to be yours. Please continue to use me for your glory. In Jesus' name, amen.'

Exhausted by the effort, Kenan struggled back into bed. The Job's comforters quietly left the room. There was nothing left for them to say. Jenny felt a wave of anger swelling up inside her, but it was mingled with amazement and thanksgiving too – amazement at a God who could give such grace to a very ordinary Christian so that he could, with Jesus, turn the other cheek and take the sinner's place. That kind of grace released power that made the power of all Turkey's revolutions look paltry in comparison.

The doctors at St Mary's had given strict instructions that Kenan was to return for a check-up should any major illness develop, even though it might seem quite unconnected with the transplanted kidney. Very reluctantly, on 15 May, Kenan and Jenny flew off to London to visit the hospital. For most of Kenan's friends it was just like another routine check-up; they had become used to seeing the two making these regular trips. They expected to see Kenan back a few days later, his normal, cheerful self, once again exuding bounce and vitality.

The first time Kenan had flown to London everyone had felt they were saying goodbye to him for the last time. Only he himself had really believed that he would come back alive. This time, on what was his final trip, the roles were reversed. Everyone thought that Kenan would be back, except Kenan himself. As the plane circled high over Istanbul's towering palaces and minarets before heading for England, Kenan had a strange feeling that he was never going to see his beloved Turkey again.

In London the doctor was reassuring. He started Kenan on a course of treatment, and soon the fever began to come down. Kenan and Jenny began to think they would be back in Istanbul sooner than they had expected, but on Sunday night, 19 May, Kenan was suddenly taken ill again. In the early hours of Monday morning he collapsed into a semi-conscious state. Jenny immediately called an ambulance, which rushed him to King's College Hospital. She knew that there was something terribly wrong, but was reassured that in the hospital he would have expert care.

'Please wait outside one moment, Mrs Araz,' the doctor said kindly, as Kenan was quickly wheeled into the Casualty Department. Jenny sat down to wait. After a few moments the doors of Casualty burst open and the doctor came running out with some serious-faced nurses to fetch equipment and more doctors. Soon the doors opened again and the doctor came out, looking grave.

'I'm afraid I have bad news for you, Mrs Araz. Your husband has just died.'

Kenan? Dead? For a moment the words had a totally numbing effect, as if they were intended for someone else. They were foreign, strange, ugly words. What had they to do with her . . . ?

For the next few days Jenny lived in a blur, almost as if the events were happening to someone else – the condolences, the interminable ringing of the telephone, the telegrams, the awkward silences, the endless cups of hot tea, the outpouring of warm sympathy and love from so many Christian friends, the retelling of the events immediately preceding Kenan's death, the funeral in the cemetery in south-east London where a wild profusion of spring flowers were a sudden agonising reminder of moments enjoyed together wandering in the parks of Istanbul.

Jenny clung to one basic fact – Kenan was with Jesus. Kenan's favourite verse kept coming back to her:

'And this is the testimony: God has given us eternal life,

and this life is in his Son. He who has the Son has life; he who does not have the Son of God does not have life.'

Jenny remembered the longing that Kenan had experienced to be with Christ during those long days of pain and frustration preceding his transplant operation. Now those longings were fulfilled. That Kenan was with Christ Jenny had not the slightest doubt. But how hard it was for those who remained!

Through the numbing sorrow of those early traumatic days following Kenan's death, and before the long process of real grief had scarcely had time to begin, Jenny experienced through the tears many signs of God's love, many instances that assured her that *her* Big Father knew what he was doing and was working out his intricate yet perfect plan. Kind friends provided a quiet and peaceful home. Jenny had hardly any money, since when Kenan died they had virtually nothing in the bank, no property and no insurance policy. But Jenny soon found that the Church, the body of Christ, was her best insurance policy. Gifts started to pour in, often from people she hardly knew. In the first few weeks after Kenan's death over £1,000 came in as gifts, more than enough to cover the heavy funeral expenses and the financial burden of moving out of their flat back in Istanbul. Jenny had never experienced anything like this before and was deeply touched by this outpouring of practical love.

On 31 May, several hundred people packed into Balham Baptist Church for a memorial service. Some of Kenan's closest friends could not be there since they were in Turkey and other countries. Many who came were people who Jenny hardly knew, but so great had the number of people actively praying for Turkey now become that the news of Kenan's death quickly circulated.

One after the other, Kenan's friends stood up to testify what his life had meant to them. There was one common theme running through all that was said – Kenan's constant attitude of praise. David, who had been Kenan's best man at his wedding, and who himself had been deported from Turkey some years previously because of his witness for Christ, reminded the congregation of the verses Kenan had engraved on the inside of his wedding ring. They were 1 Thessalonians 5:16-18 : 'Be joyful always; pray continually; give thanks in all circumstances, for this is God's will for you in Christ Jesus.'

So Kenan was remembered not for his great successes, not for the number of Muslims he had led to Christ, not for his involvement in translation work, but for the fact that he had learned the secret of how to give thanks to God in *all* circumstances.

George Verwer, who gave the main message of the evening, captured something of the struggle to part from one with such a praising heart when he said:

'Kenan is with the Lord. And we must never cling to that which Jesus is determined to take, hard as it is to let go. It's hard to let go of loved ones. I know people who have loved ones who died ten years ago and who have still not let go. Not so with those of us who know the Lord Jesus Christ. Kenan is *with the Lord.*'

And so, for Jenny, the process of 'letting go' began. Just as growing together in marriage over the years had been a process, so the experience of 'letting go', of moving apart, was a process, a process of grieving which was to continue for months and years to come.

Staying at the Wooderson's home on the Isle of Wight at the beginning of June, Jenny found a quiet and sympathetic haven where grief could begin to work its own strange power. Beyond the sheltered little garden, with its well-cared-for mass of early summer blooms, yachts swung and bobbed at their moorings in Wootton Harbour, the tinkling of loose halyards on aluminium masts contrasting with the steady rustle of the wind through the trees.

This is what death is like, thought Jenny: a small boat coming back to the shelter of the harbour and putting down its anchor. The storms are over now. The battering of the waves is finished. Death is not a shipwreck; more like coming home to harbour, just as the navigator originally planned the voyage.

Down in Turkey to wind up her affairs a few weeks later,
Jenny found the going much tougher. There were too many
memories. The day after she arrived in Istanbul she received a message from some of Kenan's relatives: 'Tell
Jenny that we are wearing black and we want to fit her out
with some black dresses.'

Black dresses! Jenny burst into tears. Black meant that
Kenan was in the grave, under the ground. It meant
hopelessness, despair. No, she could not wear black, however much local customs might demand it. Though Kenan's
corpse might be rotting, the real Kenan was with Jesus. She
wrote back to the relatives, trying to explain why death had
lost its sting. She knew what a shock the letter would be in
the conservative Midyat culture, where a death in the family was generally followed by a rigorous programme of
mourning, and where it was considered shameful indeed to
break the pattern.

For Kenan's immediate family his death came as a tremendous shock, all the more marked as it was so unexpected. Yet through Kenan's witness several of them now
had quite a different view of death. They sorrowed deeply,
but not like those who 'have no hope' (1 Thess. 4:13).

On 20 July 1975, a memorial service was held for Kenan
in a large Armenian church in Istanbul. The church was
packed with several hundred people – the largest gathering
of true believers in Turkey that had taken place for many
years. It was an oppressively hot, sticky evening, and the
two large fans whirling overhead did little to cool the
crowded building. As the great congregation rose to sing
hymn of praise after hymn of praise, many of them Kenan's
own favourite hymns of rejoicing that he had so often
asked to be sung in the local fellowship, there were some
present who, in the normal course of events, would rarely
meet for worship together; indeed, if the truth were told,
would hardly talk to each other. Yet here they were one,
giving thanks together for what God had done in the life of
one very ordinary individual. So in death, as in life, Kenan

was forever the peacemaker, building bridges where others were apparently intent on building walls.

In the congregation on that hot summer's evening was Shamun – the same Shamun who was from Midyat and who had come to Christ at about the same time as Kenan. Sadly Shamun had drifted far from God over the intervening years. But there was something else that had pained Kenan and Jenny very much. For various reasons a rift had developed between them and Shamun, and he had avoided coming to see them for some years. How many times Kenan and Jenny had brought this to God in prayer, that Shamun might be brought back to the Shepherd who loved him so much, and that their own personal fellowship with him might be restored.

Despite this break in their relationship, Shamun had been shocked to hear of Kenan's sudden death. Now here he was at the memorial service, listening carefully as speaker after speaker rose to share what Kenan's life had meant to them, of the way in which God could take any man and by the power of his Holy Spirit make him into the kind of person that he wanted him to be. As Shamun sang the old familiar hymns and heard Christ being uplifted, his mind turned back to the tremendous times of fellowship he had enjoyed with Kenan in the earlier years, to the hours they had spent on their knees together, to the times when they had witnessed together to Muslims. Yet his life seemed barren and meaningless since he had drifted away from God. He had excellent health, a good job and plenty of money, but few friends. Yet here was Kenan, with shocking health for much of his life, no money, often jobless, and yet a church full of people had come from all over Turkey to give thanks for what God had accomplished through him.

A verse of scripture from one of the speakers completed the penetration of Shamun's armour of self-defence:

'What good is it for a man to gain the whole world, yet forfeit his soul?'

Inside Shamun something hard and unyielding suddenly snapped and his eyes filled with tears. As he sat silently

weeping in the crowded pew, God touched him and dealt
with him and restored him. As he stood with the hundreds
of other Turkish believers to sing the last hymn, for Shamun the words had a new reality and meaning:

'Face to face I will see him beyond the stars
Face to face I will see the Lord in his glory . . . .'

It will never be known exactly what took place between
God and Shamun on that July evening in 1975, but what is
clear is that Kenan's memorial service was for him a turning back to God from a spiritual wilderness. So in death as
in life it was as if Kenan was continuing a ministry of constantly reaching out to others, always encouraging, continually exhorting.

A few weeks after Kenan's memorial service Shamun
was in a taxi with three others on the road from Mardin to
Midyat. The taxi, travelling at high speed, was involved in a
head-on collision with a petrol tanker. All the passengers,
including Shamun, were killed instantly.

God did not allow Shamun to reach Midyat but took him
as he journeyed. God took Kenan as he too was on a journey. The Turkish Church itself is on a journey, a journey
often full of persecution and suffering, involving the death
of many, seemingly before their time. Yet, it is never a
Church of despair, because that great architect and master
builder, God himself, Kenan's Big Father, is putting the
stones in place.

In Midyat, in the area at the edge of the town that the
local people still call 'Little Lake', the old grey house with
its massive stone walls still stands where it has stood for
the last hundred years. It has continued to stand because
each great stone slab was carefully and individually shaped
before being put into place with such toil and effort. Love,
faith and perseverance went into its building. But, inevita-
bly, one day it will be pulled down or destroyed.

However, God's building in Turkey, his Church, will
never be destroyed. The building is not yet finished. The
scaffolding is still up. There are gaps in the walls that only

more stones can fill. But gradually the structure is taking shape according to the architect's plans.

What is really needed are more Kenans to fill the gaps. Where will they come from? Perhaps we can be involved in that more than we ever realised . . . .

Epilogue

Since Kenan died, several other Turkish believers have been snatched to heaven at a young age, seemingly before their time. Several of these have been from Muslim families.

Soner was a student in Ankara when he professed faith in Christ through the witness of a local believer. A few months later he was killed on the platform of a suburban station as the rush-hour crowd surged forward to board a train.

At about the same time, another Muslim called Mustafa came to Christ in Ankara. Shortly afterwards, Mustafa was killed in a *dolmush* as he travelled to visit his fiancée.

Then there was Mine. She was still an atheist studying in Ankara when Soner and Mustafa died. It was not until she went to study in Cambridge that the kingdom of God broke into her life. In the summer of 1981 Mine went to serve as a cook at a Christian camp on England's south coast. There she drowned under mysterious circumstances.

The mind goes back over 160 years of mission work during which thousands of men and women have given their lives in order that people like Kenan, Soner, Mustafa and Mine might hear of God's love. Giving up promising careers, often forfeiting opportunities of money-making or early marriage, they buried themselves in language study and came to remote corners of Anatolia to labour for a while, only to be ambushed by robbers, or be caught up in a massacre, or succumb to the latest wave of cholera or typhoid. Browse through the old missionary reports and one's mind boggles at the human cost of replacing Turkey's missing candlesticks.

The *old* mission reports? What about David who, a few years ago, went to share the gospel in Turkey, and was gunned down by terrorists at the age of twenty-six, leaving a widow expecting their first baby?

Is God only a Big Father when everything goes according to plan?

By the tidy standards of western efficiency, the growth of the Church in Turkey has certainly seemed quite haphazard and inefficient. If we were factory managers, interested in rapid growth and maximal use of available personnel, *we* would never do it quite like that!

So, in what kind of 'efficiency' is God interested? The Bible gives us some clues: the people of Israel wandering in the desert for forty years, taking the long route to the promised land because God was patiently teaching them some crucial lessons about themselves along the way; Joseph, sold as a slave and languishing for years in an Egyptian prison because God had a greater plan for him; John the Baptist, faithfully preparing the way for Jesus Christ, then thrown into jail and executed at the prime of life when the daughter of Herodias danced so well at a birthday party; Stephen, chosen to serve at tables, yet doing wonders and miracles among the people, seemingly at the height of an effective ministry when he was cut down by a hail of stones; James, the brother of John, executed so early in his ministry that the New Testament hardly tells us what he did, in contrast to Peter who, after being imprisoned during the same persecution, was dramatically released by an angel.

Biblical faith is about being sure of what you hope for and certain of what you do *not* see. The sower's job is to continue to sow the seed of the kingdom, even when the main harvest still lies unseen in the future.

And the hall-mark of God's efficiency is quality of life – Christ-like character that can only be produced by the constant pruning work of the Holy Spirit, whether in the life of the individual or in the life of the Church. God is adding flowers to his flower-garden each day and every single one is unique in its beauty and in its character. The efficiency of God is directed towards how the flowers are going to be in his garden, the extent to which they begin to express the fragrance of Christ himself – and *that* is a fragrance that can never be manufactured artificially.

Today Jenny is happily remarried to a pastor and lives in London. Kenan's brother and sisters are scattered across several countries. During the late 1970s there was a mass migration of Assyrians from the little town of Midyat up to Sweden, and in 1981 Kenan's parents and his younger brother moved there as well.

Others are living now in the old missionary house in 'Little Lake' on the outskirts of Midyat. Many houses left vacant by migrating Christians have been taken over by Muslim Kurds moving in from the surrounding villages. Midyat is no longer a Christian island in a Muslim sea as the town itself takes on a more Muslim character. The old Protestant church building still stands, filled with rows of dusty pews. At the back a small circle of chairs forms a ring around a paraffin stove. From time to time the chairs will be filled as a few elderly believers thumb the pages of the well-worn hymnals, and the church tower echoes again to the sound of well-loved hymns.

Watch the little group disperse after the service as they slowly wend their way home, talk to elderly Assyrians in their homes as they tell you how their families are faring in Stockholm, Berlin or Amsterdam, and you may receive the impression that Christians are a dying breed in Turkey, that as the ancient Christian communities disperse so the Church in the area is dying as well.

Nothing could be further from the truth. In other parts of Turkey the Holy Spirit is doing a *new* work. Patiently but surely God is putting the new stones into place. *God* is building his Church, and the gates of hell will not prevail against it.

Glossary

Abdulhamid II
Sultan of the Ottoman Empire from 1876 until 1909. He ruled despot-
ically following the murder of Midhat Pasha for thirty years until constitutional reform was enforced in 1908 by the Young Turks, by whom
he was forcibly deposed in 1909.

Anatolia
name derived from the Greek *anatole* (sunrise). Used originally to in-
dicate all lands east of the Aegean Sea, it gradually came to be the
name of all the land known as Asia Minor. The equivalent word in
modern Turkish is *Anadolu* and designates all of Turkey in Asia.

Ankara
formerly Ancyra and Angora. Established as the capital and seat of
government of Turkey in 1924, Ankara is situated in the west central
part of Anatolia, 3,000 feet above sea level. The capital was planned as
a small European-style town but is now a large and sprawling city, the
second largest in Turkey. Visually, it is the main monument of the
Ataturk era.

Armenians
a people originating from Armenia, a kingdom once centred around
Lake Van and Mount Ararat, but now scattered all over the world.
Most of Armenia was under Ottoman rule from the sixteenth century.
It was the first community to adopt Christianity as its official religion
(c. 303 AD), forming an independent church similar to Eastern Orthodox churches in practice and doctrine, embracing the Monophysite dogma.

Assyrians
a group, known as the Suryani by the Turks, who have Syriac as their
native tongue. They do not constitute a separate race or particular
church but are those members of various churches in which the terms
'Syrian' or 'Assyrian' are used.

Ataturk (1880-1938)
literally 'Father of the Turks'. So-called from 1935 but born Mustafa

Kemal, he came to prominence in the Gallipoli campaign (1915) against the Allies, consolidating his leadership in 1919 when he became commander of the Turkish national resistance and organised the Turkish Nationalist Party. He set up in Ankara a rival government to the last Ottoman Sultan, Vahdettin, who fled Istanbul in 1922 following Kemal's victory in the War of Independence against the Greeks and the Allies. He became the first president of the new Republic of Turkey in 1923, setting the country firmly on a course of secularisation (by disestablishing Islam) and westernisation.

Chaldeans
see *Syrian Catholic Church.*

dolmush
a shared taxi or minibus that runs over a specific route, picking up and discharging passengers who all pay the same fare.

hafif
Turkish for 'light'. When applied to a person it indicates that that person does not take life or a particular situation seriously enough.

'Hamd olsun, shukur olsun!'
literally, 'May there be praise, may there be thanks!'

Injil
Arabic word for the gospel or New Testament.

Islam
Arabic for 'submission', the religion founded by the prophet Mohammed c. 611 AD. Traditionally Islam is summarised as belief in: God (Allah), his angels, his books and his apostles; the last day; and the decree of both good and evil. The two main branches of Islam were formed in 661 AD when Ali, the fourth Caliph, died: the Sunnis (orthodox) accepted the first four caliphs and the claims of the Umayyad dynasty in Damascus to take over the caliphate; the Shiites (sectarian) accepted Ali but not the preceding caliphs, believing that succession from Mohammed should have been through Ali, his son-in-law.

Istanbul
formerly Byzantium and renamed Constantinople in 330 AD, becoming the capital of the Roman Empire. It was captured by the Ottoman Turks in 1453, ending the Byzantine Empire. Istanbul (so called from 1930) is the largest city and chief port of Turkey, lying at the crossing of the east-west land route from Asia to Europe and the north-south sea route from the Black Sea to the Mediterranean.

Iznik, Council of
council held in Asia Minor in 325 AD, presided over by Emperor Constantine, at which Christ was declared fully God and fully man.

Jacobites

a Monophysite sect formed after the Council of Chalcedon in 451 AD, refusing to accept the dogma of the dual nature of Christ and believing that the divine and human in Christ were fused in a single, totally divine nature (cf. the Nestorians). In 541 AD, Jacobus Baradeus of Edessa (from whom the term Jacobite stems) was consecrated bishop of the sect. There are now less than 25,000 Jacobites in Turkey, mostly in Mardin, Midyat, Diyarbakir and Istanbul.

Kileli

a high-pitched sound made at the back of the throat, used by women throughout the Middle East at times of celebration.

Kurds

a people of Aryan stock with Turkish admixture (but ethnically distinct from Turks) inhabiting eastern Turkey (since about the seventh century BC), Armenia, northern Syria, north-eastern Iraq and north-western Iran. Their language, Kurdish, is related to Persian and their religion is mainly Sunni Islam. Officially in Turkey Kurds are not recognised (being called 'eastern compatriots' or 'mountain Turks'). All Kurds continue to press for an independent state (Kurdistan).

Millet

a Turkish word meaning 'nation', from the Arabic *milla* ('religion'). A term used to describe the division of the subjects of the Ottoman Empire according to religious allegiance. In modern Turkish the word refers to a secular multi-racial nation, but still carries some of its former emotive overtones.

Monophysites

see under Jacobites.

Nestorians

a sect named after Nestorius, the Patriach of Constantinople in the early fifth century. While believing in Christ's two distinct natures, their central doctrine insists virtually on the total humanity of Christ (cf. the Jacobites), asserting that at the crucifixion, God the Father and Holy Spirit suffered equally with him. Nestorius was declared a heretic at the Council of Ephesus in 431 AD and banished. Nestorians inhabited south-eastern Turkey (where there are now probably less than 2,000), Syria and Iraq, and established a Christian influence throughout Asia, including India and China.

Nicaea

see under Iznik.

Ottoman Empire

the Turkish Empire, largest and longest surviving of all Islamic states,

founded c. 1300 by Osman (or Othman) I, who declared himself Sultan
on the fall of the Seljuk Empire. The Empire stretched over much of
eastern Europe and North Africa, Syria and Palestine, and western
Saudi Arabia. It collapsed after the First World War.

Qur'an
the holy book of Islam, Muslims believing that it has existed eternally
in heaven and was revealed to Mohammed by the angel Gabriel.

Ramazan, fast of
called Ramadan by the Arabs (meaning 'the hot month'), the major
fast for Muslims, entailing strict fasting from sunrise to sunset during
the ninth month of the Muslim year. It is performed as a debt to God
and in gratitude for his gift of the Qur'an to man.

Sheriat
Turkish for 'law', the traditional code of Islamic law, civil or criminal,
based mainly on the Qur'an and the Hadith (traditions of
Mohammed).

Sunni Muslims
see under Islam.

Syriac
the language of ancient Syria, spoken there until the thirteenth
century. It is a branch of Aramaic, spoken still by the Assyrians of
eastern Turkey and surviving as the liturgical language of certain
eastern churches.

Syrian Catholic Church
Syrian Catholics are in communion with Rome and can be considered
the local equivalent of the Roman Catholic Church. Often known as
the Cheldani, they are more widely known as the Chaldeans. After the
Nestorian split in the seventeenth century, those who accepted
Rome's supremacy (cf. Assyrians) began to be known as the
Chaldeans, a term apparently used by Jesuit missionaries to associate
the group with the early Christian Church in Mesopotamia, which had
called itself the 'Chaldean Church'.

Syrian Orthodox Church
see Jacobites.

Young Turks
the group of army officers, fervent patriotic nationalists and founders
of the Committee of Union and Progress, who led the revolution
against Sultan Abdulhamid II in 1908, forcing him to proclaim a liberal
constitution and in 1909 deposing him in favour of his brother,
Mohammed V.

Bibliography

American Board of Commissioners for Foreign Missions Reports, 1844-1921

Ayanoğlu, Stylianos (1970) *Small Man,*Good News Publishers

Barton, J. (1908) *Daybreak in Turkey*, The Pilgrim Press, Boston

Bilezikian, Vartan (1953) *Abraham Hoja of Aintab*, Light and Life Press

Bliss, E.M. (1891) *Encyclopaedia of Missions,*Vol. 2, Funk and Wagnalls

Bostancioğlu, Annetta (1982) *Anatolia, Anatolia*

Brown, W. (1854) *History of Missions*

Bryce, Viscount (1972)*The Treatment of Armenians in the Ottoman Empire 1915-16*, G. Doniguian and Sons, Beirut

Burnaby, F. (1877) *On Horseback Through Asia Minor*, 2 Vols.

Campbell, J.A. (1906) *The Caliph's Last Heritage*, William Blackwood and Sons

Childs, W.J. (1918) *Across Asia Minor on Foot*, William Blackwood and Sons

Correspondence Respecting Protestant Missionaries and Converts in Turkey, presented to both Houses of Parliament by Command of Her Majesty, 1865

Dolapönü, M.H. (1971) *Deyr-el-umur Tarihi*, Baha Matbasi

Dolapönü, M.H. (1972) *Tarihte Mardin*, Hilâl Matbaacilik Koll. Sti.

Dwight, H.O. (1854) *Christianity in Turkey: A Narrative of the Protestant Reformation in the Armenian Church*, James Nisbet and Co.

Dwight, H.O. (1916) *The Centennial History of the American Bible Society*

Glimpses From the Life of Stephanos Sirinides, undated

Günel, Aziz (1970) *Türk Süryaniler Tarihi*, Diyarbakir

Harris, J.R. (1897) *Letters from Armenia*, James Nisbet

Hasluck, F.W. (1929) *Christianity and Islam Under the Sultans*, Clarendon Press

Hotham, David (1972) *The Turks*, John Murray Ltd

Isler, Cemil (1970) *İlçemiz Midyat*, Kutulmus Matbasi

Kidd, B.J. (1927) *The Churches of Eastern Christendom*, The Faith Press Ltd

Kostanick, H.L. (1957) *Turkish Resettlement of Bulgarian Turks*, University of California Press

Lewis, Bernard (1961) *The Emergence of Modern Turkey*, Oxford University Press

Mango, Andrew (1968) *Turkey*, Thames and Hudson

Missionary Heralds (1860-1916)

Richter, J (1910) *History of Protestant Missions in the Near East*, Oliphant, Anderson and Ferrier

Southgate, Horatio (1840) *Narrative of a Tour Through Armenia, Kurdistan, Persia and Mesopotamia*, Tilt and Bogue (2 Vols.)

Student Volunteer Missionary Union Reports, 1894, 1902, 1904 and 1910.

If you would like more information about being involved personally in God's work in Turkey, write to: Turkish Inquiries, PO Box 17, Bromley, Kent, England.